Fun-to-Make
WOODEN TOYS

Fun-to-Make
WOODEN TOYS

TERRY FORDE

Sterling Publishing Co., Inc.   New York

Published in 1986 by
Sterling Publishing Co., Inc.
Two Park Avenue
New York, N.Y. 10016

© 1986 by Terry Forde

ISBN 0-8069-6378-6

First published in Great Britain in 1986 as Fun-to-Make Wooden Toys.
Published by arrangement with David & Charles Publishers plc.
This edition available in the United States and Canada.
Printed in Great Britain.

Distributed in Canada by Oak Tree Press Ltd.
c/o Canadian Manda Group, P.O. Box 920, Station U,
Toronto, Ontario M8Z 5P9

CONTENTS

FOREWORD

If two similar toys are displayed side by side, one made from wood the other plastic, almost certainly the wooden toy will be the one most admired, even though the plastic one probably contains more detail. It was the amount of detail in such toys that disappointed me as a child, it always seemed to get in the way of my imagination. My own children provide an example which may help to clarify what I mean. When my eldest daughter was about three or four my wife brought her into the office where I was working and she promptly decided that she wanted to be a typist. My wife painted a typewriter keyboard onto an old supermarket box and my daughter played with it endlessly. That Christmas one of her presents was a toy typewriter. This delighted her until she discovered that she could not use all her fingers at once without jamming the keys. She promptly reverted back to her imagination and the box – the typewriter was never used after Christmas Day.

Wooden toys certainly have an appeal and I believe that most people would choose them providing the prices were comparable with plastic toys. Unfortunately wooden toys are usually expensive – which is where this book comes in. The most common questions people ask when they are thinking of making a wooden toy for the first time are: 'Do I need a lot of expensive tools?', 'Do I need special skills?' and 'Are the materials expensive?'. Happily the answer to all these questions is a definite *NO!*

All the toys in this book are made using a limited number of tools; a fretsaw (jigsaw), a hammer, a pair of pliers and an ordinary electric drill with a sanding disc attachment. There are occasions when a coping saw may be preferable to the fretsaw, generally on thicker wood. If you have neither, read the chapter on the toy you intend to make before buying one. If you have other tools use them, but really only these essentials are necessary.

I suppose the answer to the second question depends on how you define skills. As far as I am concerned the most important skill is measuring accurately. I'm hopeless so I check and recheck *before* I cut. The only tool you will need to learn how to use is the fretsaw (jigsaw). A little practice will certainly make you at least as proficient as I am. Having taken the trouble to measure accurately, it makes sense to cut to the line you have drawn. This is not as difficult as some people think, providing you are not rushing. So start the toy with plenty of time in hand.

Toys by their very nature are small and this keeps the overall cost of expensive materials to a very economical level. It is also possible to use wood off-cuts, which are very cheap, for making many of the toys in this book. It is therefore easy for the complete beginner with only a couple of tools to make any of these toys inexpensively and to a very high standard.

Some of the toys are more complex than others but none are difficult. The castle was the first toy I ever made, so don't feel inhibited if you want to have a go at a larger or more complicated toy at your first attempt. I think the most daunting project is the Alice Chess Set, but once you start, you will be amazed at how easy the woodwork part is, and find the majority of the work in the painting. Of course you only need to try making one piece at first.

So choose a toy and get started.

HOW TO DO IT

This is a toy-making book not a wood-working book so I don't intend to go into any woodworking techniques or the contrasting merits of various tools or materials. I only intend to describe *my* methods and the tools and materials *I* use.

Tools

Fretsaw (Jigsaw)
The most important tool as far as this book is concerned is the fretsaw (jigsaw) (see fig 1). The fretsaw does not require any strength and is therefore an ideal tool for use by women and children and, since it can be used sitting down, some partially disabled people will be able to use it without discomfort. The fretsaw is also ideal because it does not need sharpening (I hate sharpening tools, but you cannot get good results with blunt ones). When the blade gets blunt, throw it away and fit a new one – they are very inexpensive.

When I first started using the fretsaw I probably broke a blade every time I turned a corner. The secret is to cut *around* the corner rather than twisting the blade or better still cut into the corner from both directions. The blade is fitted into the saw with the teeth pointing down and the saw is used with the handle

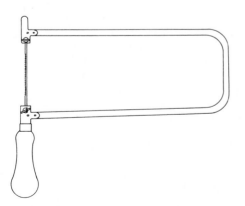

Fig 1 Fretsaw (Jigsaw)

beneath the work. It is very important that you cut at 90° especially for the jigsaw puzzles or the pieces will not fit properly, so concentrate on getting a nice rhythm going and keep the saw perpendicular.

Try to imagine that the saw is in a fixed position and move the work rather than the saw. To start a cut in the middle of a piece of work (ie Grocer's Shop windows) drill a small hole just large enough for the blade of the fretsaw to pass through and then fit the blade into the saw.

Coping Saw
The blades of the coping saw (fig 2) are more robust than the fretsaw and thus it is better for use with thicker wood, providing a very fine finish is not required.

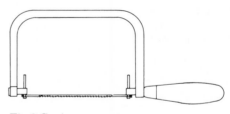

Fig 2 Coping saw

Electric Drill
Any type of drill will do as it is only used for drilling holes to pass the fretsaw blades through, or for turning the castle spires or chess pieces.

Hammer
Since you will be using small panel pins, a small hammer will be kinder to your fingers. There are various methods of holding small panel pins in order to protect your fingers; fitting them between the teeth of a comb, or pushing them through a piece of thin card to hold them until you get them started. Personally I'm not impressed with either of these methods as it always seems that I have

enough to hold without messing around with combs and cardboard. I prefer to just tap them in gently.

Pliers

These are only used for fitting the headless screws when turning wood with the drill, so any type will do.

Paint Brushes

There are two ways of choosing paint brushes, either by price or by quality. Sometimes I buy the cheapest brush available, but regret it the moment I start painting and the bristles begin to fall out. I also find that if I do not clean these cheap brushes thoroughly I have to throw them out the next time I try to use them, so for me cheap brushes are a false economy. On the other hand all the work in this book has been painted using good quality art brushes. These are comparatively expensive but I do clean them meticulously; my present brushes are about three or four years old and are still in perfect condition. I would recommend that you get a couple of good quality art brushes, one fine and one fairly wide – a long handled brush is good for getting into normally inaccessible corners.

Non-essential tools
Craft knife

These are very inexpensive and available in model shops. They can be used for cutting cardboard for jigsaw puzzle boxes, or the plastic sheet used for the glass in the doll's house windows – scissors will do just as well.

Files

I have not used these as much for the toys in this book as I did for the toys in my previous book. Although they can be handy, I now tend to use sandpaper wrapped around a piece of wood.

Materials
Wood

In the previous book I made all the toys from either ¼in (6mm) or ½in (12mm) birch ply. I still advocate this even though I have occasionally deviated from it myself. During the course of making

these toys I dismantled some fitted wardrobes and it seemed silly not to use the wood. Although this could not be detected from examining the toys since the ones concerned had all been painted, it did convince me how much more pleasant it is to work with good quality materials. In places the drawings show ½in (12mm) and ¼in (6mm) ply laminated together, but if you have ¾in (18mm) ply then use it. The only reason I have shown it like this is for economy. Since the majority of the toy is made in say, ½in (12mm) and ¼in (6mm) ply, the amount of ¾in (18mm) ply you would have to buy for the very small amount needed would be very wasteful.

Glue

I only use wood glue. The one I choose is Evo-Stick Resin 'W'. I have no idea how it compares with other glues, but if ever I have tried to 'unstick' two pieces of wood the bond is never the part to break – that's strong enough for me.

Nails

Throughout the instructions I use terms such as 'nail', or 'glue and nail'. However, I don't use nails as I prefer panel pins.

Woodfiller

All panel pins should be punched below the surface. You can buy a punch but I have been using a nail with the point blunted for the past two years (I'm sure I would have lost a punch by now). The resulting hole and any other blemishes should be filled with a woodfiller prior to painting. Panel pins tend to rust and spoil the paintwork so either use a waterproof filler or put a spot of oil based primer or undercoat on the pin before filling.

Paint

All paints used must be *non-toxic*. I have found it cheaper to buy the primary colours and if I want, say, green then I mix it from blue and yellow. Several of the toys have gold paint on them and unfortunately the cheaper gold paints available in model shops are not very authentic. I use the gold paint which is used in art shops for touching up gilt

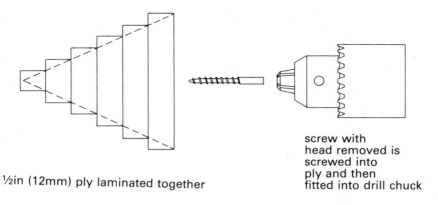

½in (12mm) ply laminated together

screw with
head removed is
screwed into
ply and then
fitted into drill chuck

Fig 3 Technique for turning spires and wheels

frames. It is not cheap but the finish is very good.

Techniques
Turning
The majority of the toys depend on the use of the fretsaw (jigsaw) and a little practice will make you proficient. The only unusual technique I have is for turning things (spires, wheels etc). I do not have a lathe so I use my electric drill (fig 3). Cut the piece you are turning as close to circular as possible (use a child's pair of compasses to make the circle as this leaves a mark in the centre). Cut the head off a thin screw about 1½in (40mm) long, tap it into the centre of the circle and tighten it by using a pair of pliers. Fit the protruding end of the screw into an electric drill. Hold the drill firmly on a table or chair and bring a piece of coarse sandpaper into contact with the edge of the disc; this will soon turn your rough circle into a perfect circle. When making wheels (eg the Cinderella coach) turn them in pairs to ensure they are exactly the same size.

To make the spires of the castle, cut discs of decreasing size and laminate them together; turn them in exactly the same way. Use very coarse sandpaper to get the correct shape and then change to a medium grade. Finally, use woodfiller to remove any small blemishes and turn with fine grade sandpaper. Since this is a dusty job, safety goggles are a good idea and obviously don't put your face in line with the rotation of the disc.

Dimensions
All the toys in this book were originally made by the author using imperial measurements. These measurements have since been converted to their *nearest* metric equivalent.

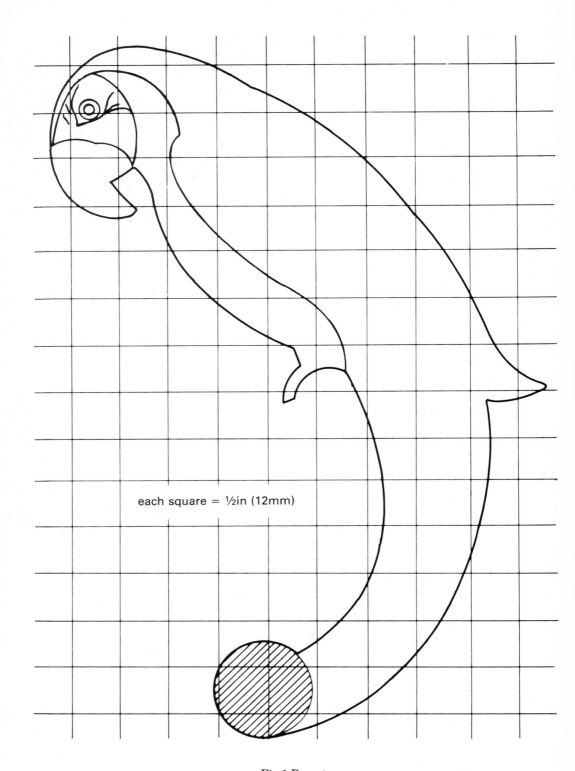

each square = ½in (12mm)

Fig 1 Parrot

ROCKING PARROTS

(shown in colour on page 70)

My previous book was published in the same week that my youngest daughter was born and included a mobile I had made ready for her. These parrots were the next toys I made.

1 Mark and cut out the parrots from ⅛in (4mm) birch ply. (see How To Do It, page 7)
2 From the ⅛in (4mm) ply cut several pieces the same shape as the bottom of the parrot's tail (shaded in fig 1), and glue them to either side of the tail until the parrot balances (you will need about four pieces on each side).
3 Sand them down and paint. Babies can detect primary colours earlier than other colours, which is why toy manufacturers use mainly primary colours, so avoid using pastel shades, green or other combinations of primary colours.

The parrots will balance on almost anything so there is no need to make a perch for them.

PANDA BOOKSHELF

(shown in colour on page 70)

My children have too many books for this little bookshelf but it is nice to keep the current favourites by the bedside in a novelty bookshelf.

1 Lightly nail two pieces of ½in (12mm) ply together.
2 Transfer the panda design on to the ply and cut out the two ends in one go (fig 2). It will probably be better to use the coping saw rather than the fretsaw (jigsaw) (see How To Do It, page 7).
3 Cut out a piece of 13×4×½in (330× 100×12mm) ply and a piece of 13×5½× ½in (330×140×12mm) ply.
4 Glue and nail these two pieces together at right angles (see fig 1).
5 Glue and nail the ends to the shelf. Tilt the shelf slightly as this prevents the books falling forwards if they are knocked.
6 Undercoat and paint the shelf.

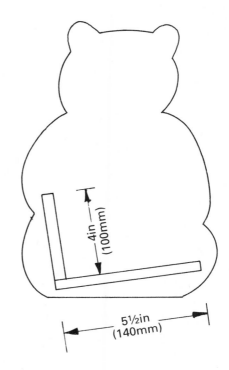

Fig 1 Position of the back and the bottom of the shelf

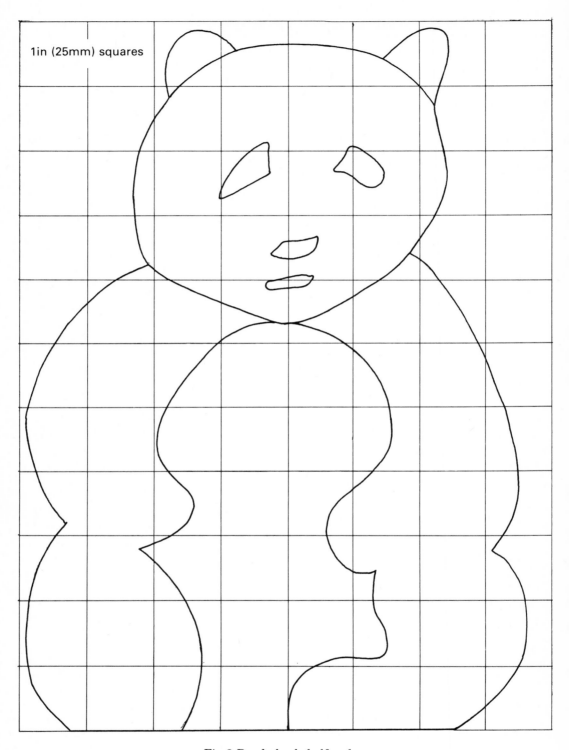

1in (25mm) squares

Fig 2 Panda bookshelf ends

TOYS FOR HANDICAPPED CHILDREN

(shown in colour on pages 34 and 52)

When I first decided to make a few toys suitable for handicapped children I thought it would be merely a matter of adapting ordinary toys by adding a handle or making the pieces more chunky. However, there are so many forms of handicap which can befall children that it is impossible to make a specific toy that is ideal for handicapped children in general. This applies equally well to ordinary children – what one child likes another doesn't.

Providing they are well made with good materials none of the toys in this book are unsuitable for handicapped children, but I leave it to the individual to decide on the suitability of a particular toy for a particular child. The underlying idea of the following toys is their flexibility in that they can easily be adapted for the child's specific needs and are intended as a guide to lead on to other ideas, rather than be well-defined toys in their own right. I've included drawings and instructions of the photographed toys in order to be consistent with the format of the book.

I don't imagine that anyone taking the trouble to make toys for handicapped children would adopt the attitude 'It'll do' or 'They won't notice the difference'. If anything, I tend to be more fussy and try to make the finished item superior to one made for ordinary children.

The original of the Three-piece Puzzle was made for a blind, mentally handicapped girl from different types of wood chosen for their different textures. It is made more effective by being painted with different textures of paint; gloss, eggshell and water-based.

At first sight some of the pictures in the Alphabet Puzzles probably appear an unusual choice. These two puzzles are samples taken from a full alphabet I originally painted on cards several years ago for my eldest daughter. The idea was to give a slightly wider scope than the usual ABC books. For instance, in the 'H' puzzle (fig 2a), the child sees a horse but there is also a highwayman. The idea of putting the alphabet into puzzles is to extend the concentration period of the child, since children learn much more readily when they don't know they are being taught.

Up to this point they are probably alright for ordinary children, but for a mentally handicapped child, you could retain the puzzle idea, but revert to a more simple 'A for apple', 'B for ball' for the content. Alternatively, for a child with poor manual dexterity the drawings may be suitable, but problems may occur fitting the pieces together. So, rather than having interlocking pieces, use pieces that slide together as in the 'S' puzzle (fig 2b). In both cases I've made the puzzle to fit into its own tray, which makes it easier for the child. Also, the pieces do not get lost if the puzzle is put away completed. If you are brave enough to make a full alphabet, when the child has outgrown them they would make a nice donation to a toy library.

The Noughts and Crosses game (Tic-tac-toe) is intended for a child who may have difficulty handling small objects: the chunky pieces should help the problem.

Three-piece Puzzle

The equilateral triangle, square and circle were chosen because it doesn't matter which way the pieces are orientated they will still fit, making it easier for the child – providing they are drawn and cut accurately.

1 Cut out the three shapes (fig 1) from ³⁄₈in (9mm) ply (see How To Do It, page 7).
2 Glue the waste wood on to a piece of hardboard.
3 Cut the three handles from, a piece of dowel 1in (25mm) diameter, a piece of 1×1in (25×25mm) wood, and a piece of triangular fillet – or cut a square piece in half.

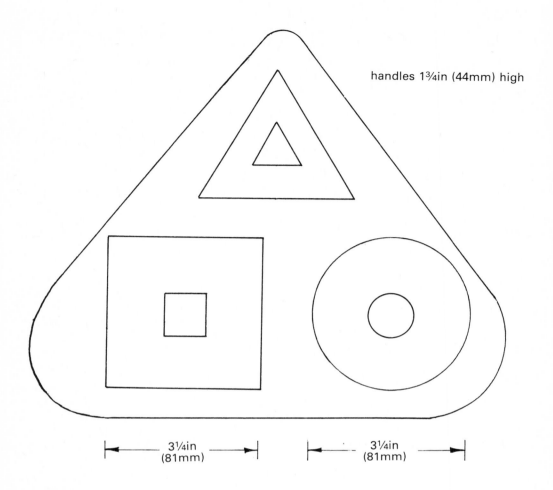

handles 1¾in (44mm) high

3¼in (81mm)

3¼in (81mm)

Fig 1 Three-piece puzzle

4 Drill a pilot hole for a screw through the three pieces and counter-sink them. Glue and screw the pieces to their handles.
5 Paint them with various colours and types of paint (see How To Do It, page 8). Harder puzzles of the same type can be made by increasing the number of pieces but still using regular polygons, later perhaps trying irregular shapes or smaller pieces.

Alphabet Puzzles
1 Seal the wood with a thin coat of varnish.
2 Either paint the pictures directly on to the wood (figs 2a and 2b), or cut them out of magazines and stick them on to the varnished wood.
3 Cut the puzzle up into either interlocking or slide-together pieces (see How To Do It, page 7).
4 Glue the border on to a piece of hardboard.

½in (12mm) squares

Fig 2a H puzzle

½in (12mm) squares

Fig 2b S puzzle

Noughts and Crosses (Tic-tac-toe)

1 Cut out five noughts and five crosses (fig 3a) from fairly thick wood, say ½in (12mm) or thicker (I used 1in (25mm)) (see How To Do It, page 7).

2 Glue strips of wood on to a square piece of ½in (12mm) ply to form the board (fig 3b) – they help to retain the pieces in the squares even if the board is accidentally knocked while playing.

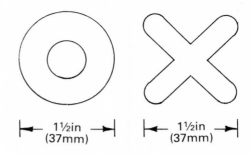

|← 1½in →|
(37mm)

|← 1½in →|
(37mm)

½in × ¼in
(12mm × 6mm)

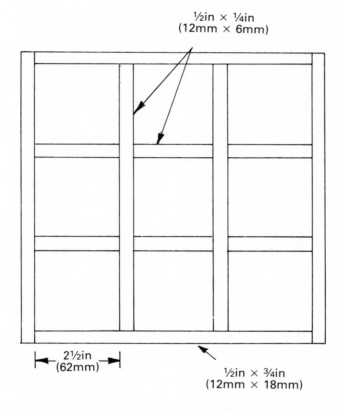

|← 2½in →|
(62mm)

½in × ¾in
(12mm × 18mm)

Fig 3 Noughts and crosses (Tic-tac-toe)

CHRISTMAS JIGSAW PUZZLES

(shown in colour on page 52)

I started making these puzzles about three days before Christmas and I wasn't really sure if I would finish them in time. As it turned out, the cardboard boxes to put them in took longer to make than the puzzle. They are both very easy to paint as the pieces are cut out first and therefore there is no need to wait for one colour to dry before applying another. Some years ago I had planned to have a holiday in Israel but eventually decided Ibiza might be a wiser choice, so if the Bethlehem scene has a hint of Ibiza Old Town that's the reason why.

Both Puzzles

1 Cut a piece of ⅜in (9mm) birch ply and a piece of ⅛in (3.2mm) hardboard to the overall size of the puzzle 13½×10in (342×253mm).

2 Give the ply a thin coat of varnish and allow it to dry. This is to seal the wood so you can transfer the design without staining the wood.

3 Transfer the design on to a piece of paper the same size as the puzzle. This will eventually be used for the picture on the lid of the box.

4 Using this full sized drawing and carbon paper transfer the design on to the wood.

5 Cut along all the heavy lines. Some of these (i.e. the lines indicating sand dunes in fig 1) are only decorative and do not produce separate pieces. Do not cut out the eyes of the Kings (fig 2); paint them in at the end as they are a bit small for separate pieces. Put the pieces back in the form of a puzzle as you cut them or it will be very difficult to reassemble the puzzle without colours. All the shaded parts of the Bethlehem puzzle (fig 1), the windows, the doors and the star are to be cut

out and discarded.

6 For the Bethlehem puzzle (fig 1), mark out the position of the star on the hardboard and glue a small piece of kitchen foil on to it. Place the outer part of the puzzle on to the hardboard and mark the outline. Either paint this internal area gold (see How To Do It, page 8) or as I did, glue gold Christmas paper on to the hardboard. When the puzzle is completed it looks as though the star is shining and there are lights on in the houses.

Glue the outer part of the puzzle on to the hardboard.

7 Use the lid off an old jar as a pallet and mix a drop of paint with some varnish. Paint the individual pieces. Mixing the paint with the varnish colours the wood but allows the grain to show through and is very effective.

8 Either buy a cardboard box big enough to take the puzzle or better still, custom make one. I probably gave the wrong impression earlier when I said it took longer to make the box than to make the puzzle. It was mainly because I could paint individual pieces of the puzzle without my daughter knowing what they were, but I had to stop work and hide the box every time she came in the kitchen – which seemed like every two minutes.

Make an ordinary cardboard box from artist card and then glue the paper picture on to the lid – this is the point where it needs to be kept out of sight of prying eyes. Stretch cling-film over the lid of the box and hold it in place with adhesive tape. Use Christmas wrapping paper to decorate around the picture and the sides of the lid. It isn't necessary to make a box, but if it is for a Christmas present it does give it the final finishing touch.

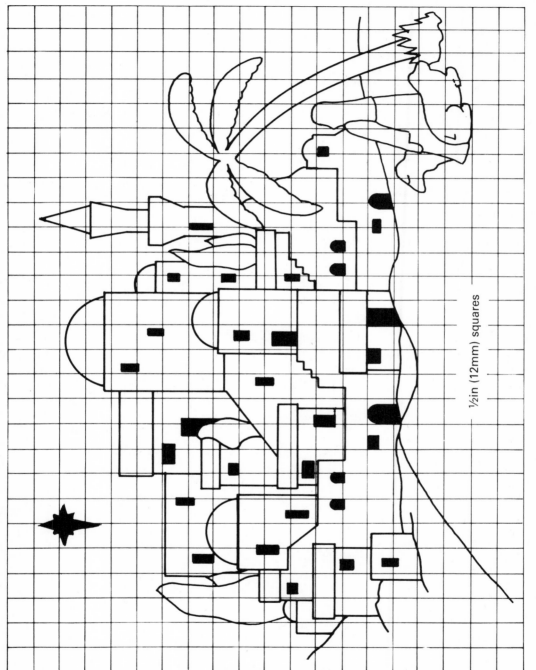

½in (12mm) squares

Fig 1 Bethlehem puzzle

½in (12mm) squares

Fig 2 Three kings puzzle

TOWER OF HANOI PUZZLE

(shown in colour on page 52)

I made this toy one Christmas and then could not decide which age group it was suitable for so I wrapped it without a name tag and left it under the tree. I might have known that my middle daughter, Ulenka, would open it and claim it as her own. But I need not have worried as everybody played with it,

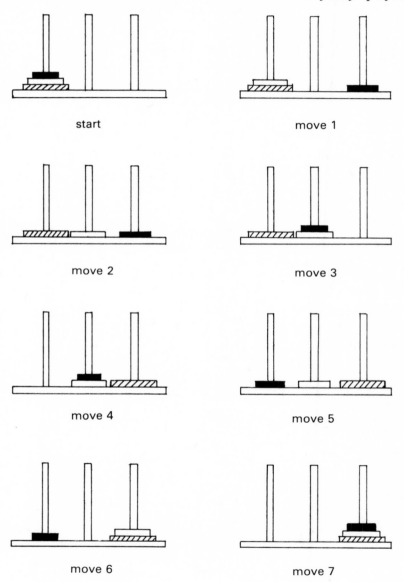

Fig 1 Tower of Hanoi puzzle using only three rings

Small ring ⅞in (22mm) diameter each ring increases in diameter by ⅜in (9mm)
therefore ring 2 = 1¼in (31mm) diameter

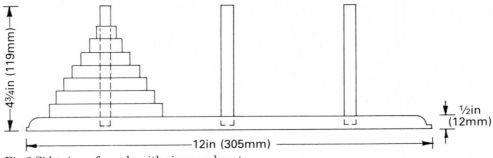

Fig 2 Side view of puzzle with rings and posts

Fig 3 Top view of puzzle showing position of holes

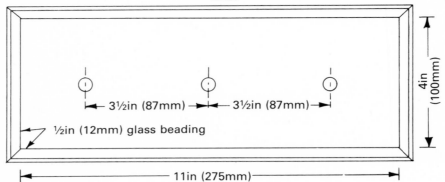

including the grown ups. The children soon mastered it and then took great delight in laughing at the grown ups who couldn't do it.

The idea of the game is to transfer all the rings, one at a time, from the pole on one side to the pole on the other side without placing any ring on a smaller one. I've calculated that to move all seven rings takes a minimum of one hundred and twenty seven moves (see diagram for how to do it with three rings fig 1). I have personally never managed to complete it since I either lose count or lose concentration and make a wrong move. If you want to try it with fewer rings the minimum number of moves are:

3 rings—7 moves;
4 rings—15 moves;
5 rings—31 moves;

6 rings—63 moves and
7 rings—127 moves
. . . anyone for 8 rings?

1 Cut out the rings and stand from ½in (12mm) ply (fig 2).
2 Drill holes in the stand for the ⅜in (9mm) dowel (fig 3) and drill slightly larger holes in the rings to enable them to slide on the poles easily.
3 I used ½in (12mm) glazing bead (available in DIY shops) to cover the end grain of the ply.
4 Glue in the dowels and varnish the stand.
5 Undercoat and then paint the rings in various colours. Use a piece of dowel to hold the rings while painting, then you can paint both sides at once rather than wait for one to dry first.

DOLL'S MUSIC BOX PIANO

(shown in colour on page 70)

The instructions for this music box piano are a bit like the old-fashioned recipe for rabbit pie which began 'First catch your rabbit' only in this case, it's 'First get your musical movement'. These are available at most model shops or can be bought by mail order through advertisements in craft magazines. The last time I looked there were over a hundred different tunes so there is quite a good selection. I have made two pianos, one playing The Entertainer, the other, Für Elise. The movements do come in different sizes which is why I advise you to get the movement before beginning. The movement I used in this piano was a Reuge $\frac{1}{18}$ B movement with wire brake (size $2\frac{1}{16} \times 1\frac{3}{4} \times \frac{7}{8}$in $(51 \times 44 \times 23$mm). The brake is to stop the music when the lid is closed.

Don't be frightened of having to bend the wood around the sides of the piano as the wood used for the sides and the soundboard is only $\frac{1}{16}$in (2mm) thick and it bends very easily. This wood is available from model shops; you can buy it even thinner, but the thinner it gets the more expensive it becomes.

I chose to make a baby grand rather than a grand because this is the same shape as our own piano and it made the designing much easier having a full sized one to copy from. I have made the lid in one piece and omitted the music stand because this is a toy rather than a model and I expected it to take some rough treatment.

1 Cut out the shaded area (fig 1) and the bottom of the piano which is the same shape but without the cut-outs. Also note that the bottom is shorter than the top. Mark the position of the movement and drill any necessary holes.
2 Cut out the four pieces for the trinket box and drill two holes for the lid stay. Glue and nail the sides together.
3 Cut out the shaded area (fig 2) which is the left side of the piano. The right hand side of the piano is the same shape but only $3\frac{1}{4}$in (82mm) long.
4 Cut out the side piece at the top of the piano which is $1 \times 1\frac{3}{4} \times \frac{1}{4}$in $(25 \times 44 \times 6$mm) ply.
5 Fix the sides and trinket box to the top and bottom of the piano.
6 Glue the $8 \times 2\frac{3}{4}$in $(200 \times 69$mm) piece of $\frac{1}{4}$in (6mm) ply on to the bottom of the piano.
7 Make the keyboard cover. The hinge is merely a panel pin tapped through the sides of the piano into small pre-drilled holes in the cover (fig 3).
8 Cut out the $\frac{1}{16}$in (2mm) thick soundboard which is the total shape shown in fig 1. Since you may need access to the musical movement, cut this into two pieces. (I divided it between the movement compartment and the trinket box.) Glue the trinket box piece in place and screw the movement cover in place. One screw is all that is needed as the screws for the hinges will hold the soundboard down.
9 With the soundboard in place glue the $\frac{1}{16}$in (2mm) sides of the piano in place. Placing the wood in water makes it even easier to bend. Glue the sides in place *before* cutting to shape with a craft knife. This makes it easier to match the curved sides at the front of the piano. The sides should be covered in two pieces making the join at the right hand side where the piano sides turn sharply.
10 Fit the musical movement. You will need to drill a small hole for a piece of thick wire to pass through to connect to the wire brake of the movement. This can be the most fiddly part. On the first piano I made, I bent the wire perfectly the first time I tried, but on this one I made about ten attempts before I got it right.
11 Make the three legs from $\frac{1}{2} \times \frac{1}{2}$in $(13 \times 13$mm) wood and glue in place.
12 Make the pedals as shown in fig 4 and glue in place.
13 Make the stay for the lid from $\frac{1}{4}$in

Fig 1 Plan view of piano showing top and
bottom layers

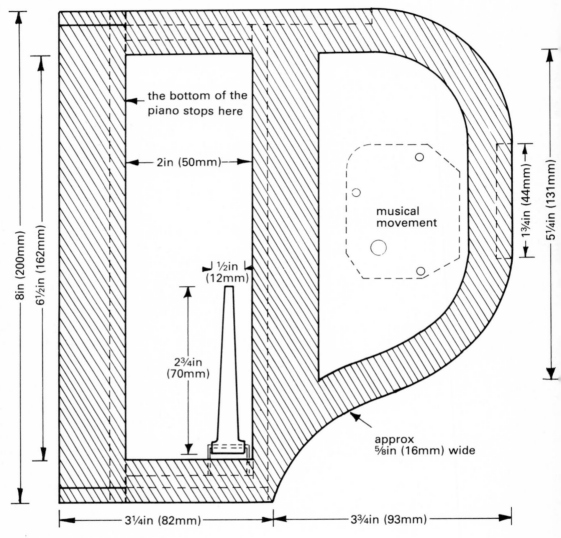

shaded area represents the top layer of the piano before
the ¹⁄₁₆in (2mm) thick soundboard is fitted

the bottom of the
piano stops here

2in (50mm)

½in
(12mm)

2¾in
(70mm)

musical
movement

1¾in (44mm)

5¼in (131mm)

approx
⅝in (16mm) wide

8in (200mm)

6½in (162mm)

3¼in (82mm)

3¾in (93mm)

(6mm) ply and drill a small hole through
it for a thick piece of wire to pass through.
The wire is bent and fitted into the pre-
drilled holes of the trinket box once it has
been varnished.

14 Varnish all of the piano. I used walnut
varnish giving the piano several thin
coats and sanding it down between each
one.

15 Line the bottom of the trinket box with
felt or a similar material.

16 Paint a piece of the ¹⁄₁₆in (2mm) ply
white for the keyboard and then paint in
the black keys. Glue the whole of the
keyboard in place.

17 Fit the lid to the piano using small
hinges.

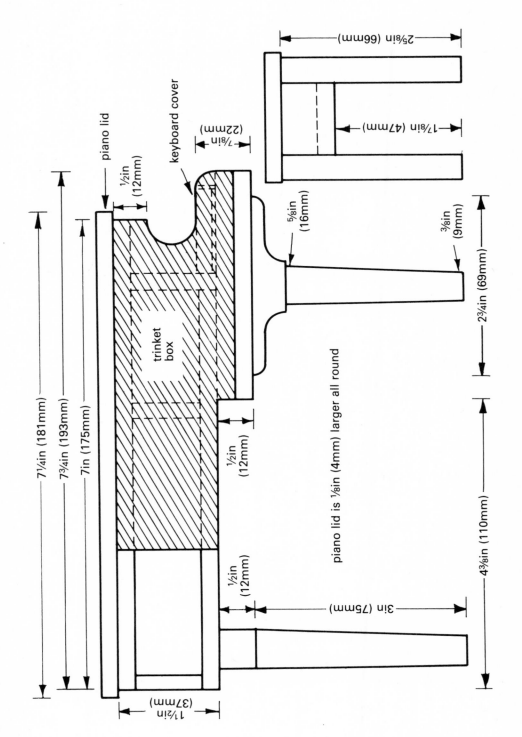

Fig 2 Side view of piano showing left and right sides

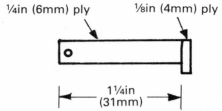

¼in (6mm) ply   ⅛in (4mm) ply

1¼in
(31mm)

Fig 3 Keyboard lid

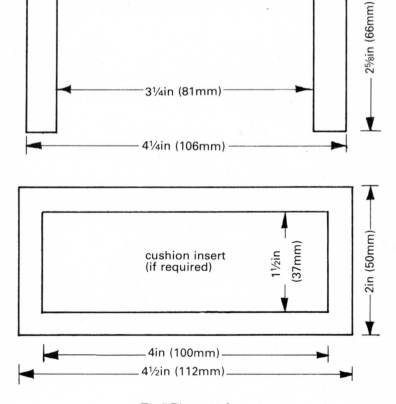

2in (50mm)

3in (75mm)

1in
(25mm)

Fig 4 Pedals for the piano

Piano Stool

I made the piano to the scale needed for a normal 11in (280mm) doll — obviously she needs somewhere to sit. Once again I used our duet stool as a model.

1 Cut out the four legs from ½×½in (13×13mm) wood and the four sides from ¼in (6mm) ply as in fig 5.

2 If a cushion is required cut out the centre part of the seat and wrap a piece of cloth around it.

3 Varnish the stool including the surround of the seat.

4 Refit the centre of the seat and glue it to the legs of the stool. This completes the toy.

2⅝in (66mm)

3¼in (81mm)

4¼in (106mm)

cushion insert
(if required)

1½in
(37mm)

2in (50mm)

4in (100mm)

4½in (112mm)

Fig 5 Piano stool

CINDERELLA'S COACH

(shown in colour on page 34)

I was probably suffering from an overdose of pantomime when I decided to make this toy. The pantomime production I took my children to see was only a small local one but the company had managed to get a real horse to pull the coach on to the stage. This really impressed the children although the actors looked a bit apprehensive. All children get carried away with the audience participation part of pantomimes when they have to shout out 'Look out behind you', 'Oh no it's not' and 'Oh yes it is' – they really get caught up in the story. Making the toy was very easy and the children enjoy playing with it, but I've noticed that they act out the pantomime rather than the fairy story.

1 Transfer the design of the coach (fig 1) on to ½in (12mm) birch ply and laminate it to another ½in (12mm) thickness to make a total thickness of 1in (25mm) (see How To Do It, page 8).
2 Cut out the shape with the fretsaw and drill the holes for the ¼in (6mm) axles (see How To Do It, page 7).

3 Transfer the horses, Cinderella, the mice, the pumpkin and the wheels (figs 2a, 2b and 3), (see How To Do It, page 9 for the wheels) on to ½in (12mm) ply and cut them out.
4 For the pole, cut out a 12×½in (305×12mm) piece of ½in (12mm) ply and drill the holes for the ¼in (6mm) dowelling (fig 4).
5 Drill a hole in the chest of each horse for the ¼in (6mm) dowelling. Do not drill all the way through the wood and make sure you drill the hole on the left side of two of the horses, and the right side of the other two.
6 Undercoat all the pieces and then paint them; this is the best bit (see How To Do It, page 8, particularly for gold paint and brushes).
7 Fit the wheels to the coach using ¼in (6mm) dowelling for the axles.
8 The horses just fit on to the 12in (305mm) pole. They are easily removed and then can be played with separately.
9 The pole is attached to the coach using two small screw hooks.

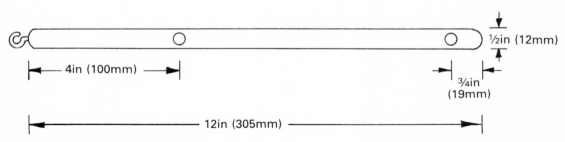

Fig 4 Coach pole to attach the horses to the coach

(Figs 1, 2a, 2b and 3 overleaf)

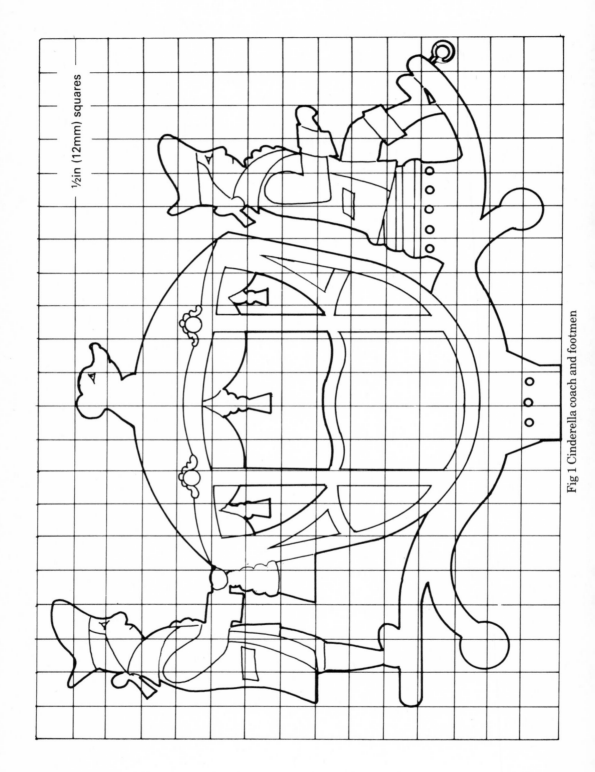

½in (12mm) squares

Fig 1 Cinderella coach and footmen

½in (12mm) squares

Fig 2a Horses

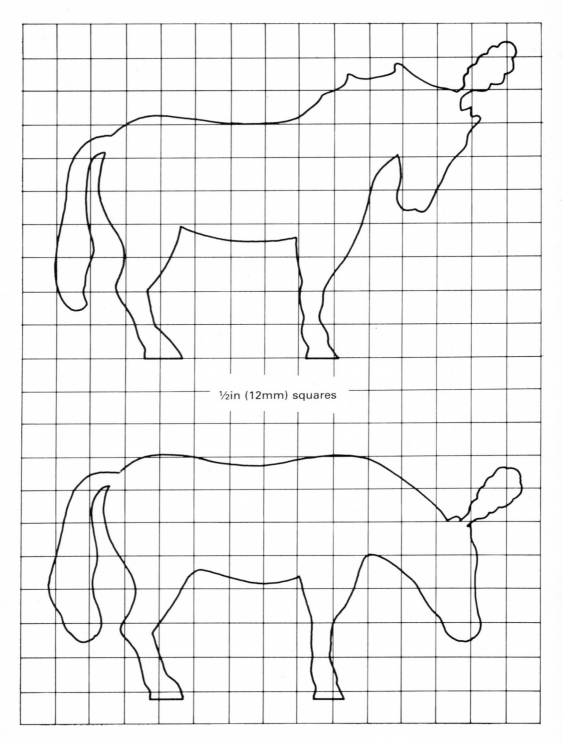

½in (12mm) squares

Fig 2b Horses

½in (12mm) squares

Fig 3 Cinderella, mice, pumpkin and wheel shape

OIL RIG

(shown in colour opposite)

This is a toy that combines several separate toys and therefore the child can get a lot of mileage out of it. The most complicated parts are the cranes, so let's get those out of the way first and then it's downhill all the way.

Crane (make two)
NB The drawings are for a right handed child. If you want one for a left handed child put the handle to raise the crane hooks (fig 7) on the left hand side.

1 Cut out the six sides of the crane cab and its roof (figs 1 and 2) from ¼in (6mm) ply. (It is a good idea to mark them in pencil so that they don't get mixed up.)
2 The dowelling used is ⅜in (9mm) so drill holes slightly larger so that it will

turn easily (fig 1). When drilling the holes place one side on top of the other to ensure they match up.
3 Glue and nail the sides and the roof together as in fig 3.
4 Cut out the four pieces for the jib (fig 4). Drill a hole through the two longest sides for the dowel and then glue and nail the pieces together. Tap in a small panel pin near the top of the jib (see fig 1) for the string to pass over.
5 Cut out a ½in (12mm) thick block of ply to fit to the bottom of the turntable (fig 5). This block enables you to have access to the strings should they break and need replacing.
6 Cut out the 3in (75mm) diameter turntable and drill a hole through its centre and into the block (see fig 6). Either drill

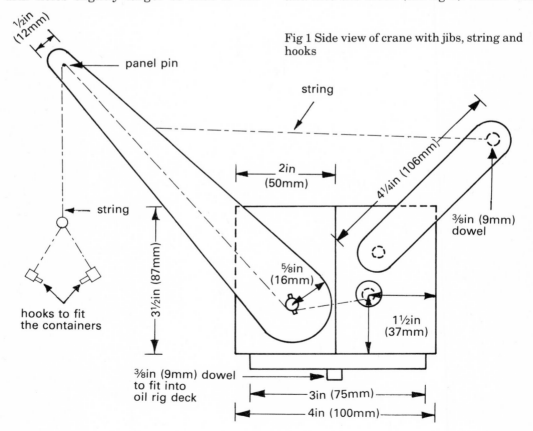

Fig 1 Side view of crane with jibs, string and hooks

½in (12mm)

panel pin

string

2in (50mm)

4¼in (106mm)

⅜in (9mm) dowel

string

3½in (87mm)

⅝in (16mm)

hooks to fit the containers

1½in (37mm)

⅜in (9mm) dowel to fit into oil rig deck

3in (75mm)

4in (100mm)

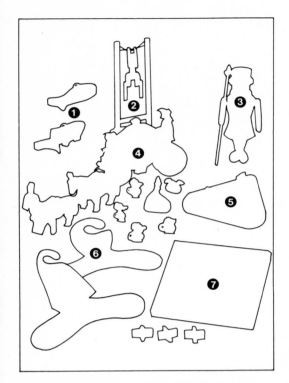

1 Fishing Game (page 128); 2 Acrobat (page 131); 3 Stacking Beefeater (page 72); 4 Cinderella's Coach, Horses, Mice and Pumpkin (page 27); 5 Three-piece Puzzle (page 13); 6 Coathangers (page 122); 7 Noughts and Crosses (tic-tac-toe) (page 17)

another ⅜in (9mm) hole through both as in fig 6 or screw the turntable to the block. This keeps the turntable fixed in position relative to the block but allows it to be removed for access.

7 Fit the block into the bottom of the crane.

8 Now is a good time to paint the cab and the jib.

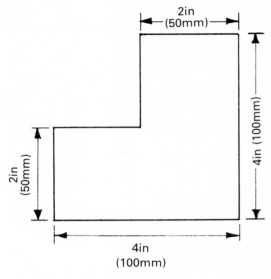

Fig 2 Crane cab roof

9 Make up the handle for raising the crane 'hooks' (fig 7).

NB The wooden spacer between the crane cab and this handle is thicker than the others to enable it to pass over the jib raising handle (fig 8).

10 Paint the inside of the handles, fit them in place and then paint the outside.

11 Fit the string in place (see fig 1).

12 The hooks are made from ⅛in (4mm) dowel fitted into ⅜in (9mm) dowel. The string is fitted by drilling a small hole in the side of the ⅜in (9mm) dowel and glueing the string into it. A small brass ring is used to connect the two small pieces of string to the main one (see fig 1). These hooks fit into holes in the containers of the supply ship and also into the drill pipes. The remainder of the oil rig is now straightforward.

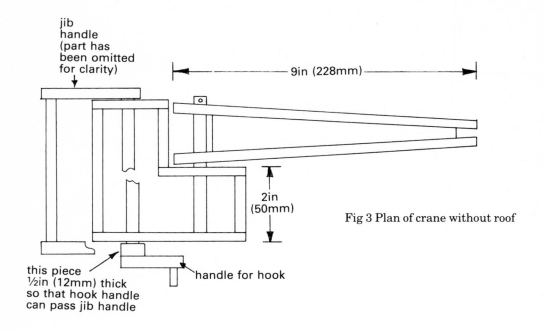

jib handle (part has been omitted for clarity)

9in (228mm)

2in (50mm)

Fig 3 Plan of crane without roof

this piece ½in (12mm) thick so that hook handle can pass jib handle

handle for hook

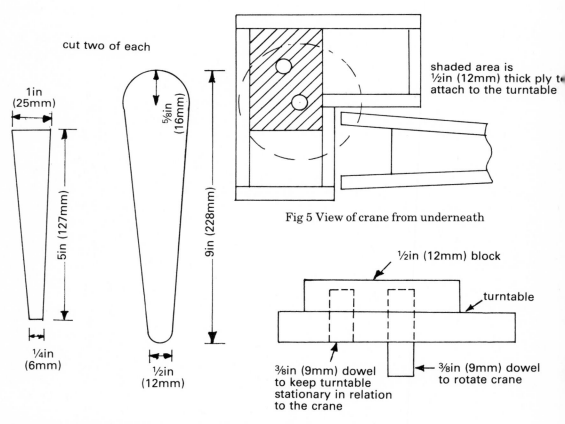

cut two of each

1in (25mm)

⅝in (16mm)

9in (228mm)

5in (127mm)

¼in (6mm)

½in (12mm)

shaded area is ½in (12mm) thick ply to attach to the turntable

Fig 5 View of crane from underneath

½in (12mm) block

turntable

⅜in (9mm) dowel to keep turntable stationary in relation to the crane

⅜in (9mm) dowel to rotate crane

Fig 4 Pieces for jib framework (cut two of each)

Fig 6 Crane turntable

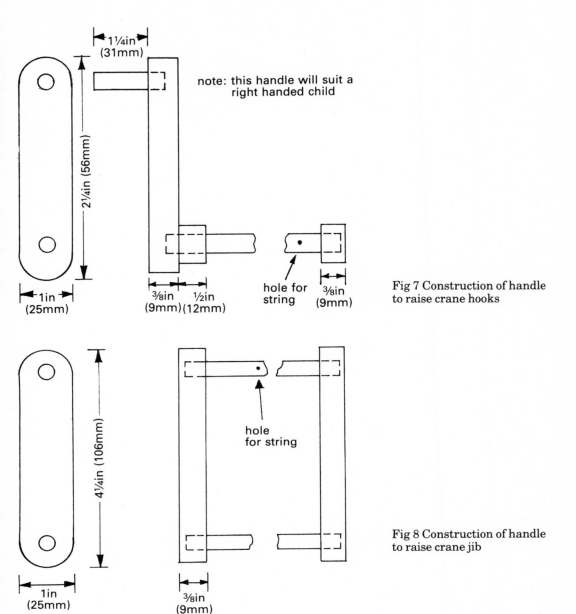

note: this handle will suit a
right handed child

hole for
string

Fig 7 Construction of handle
to raise crane hooks

hole
for string

Fig 8 Construction of handle
to raise crane jib

Crew's Quarters
1 Cut out the six sides from ¼in (6mm) ply (fig 9).
2 Glue and nail them together.
3 Cut out the roof and fix in place.
4 Drill a ⅜in (9mm) hole in the roof for the crane wherever you want to place it. I once worked on a building site and was nosing around the office when I came across the site layout featuring the tower cranes. Until I saw the drawing it had never occurred to me that the cranes had been arranged in such a way that they covered the whole site. Perhaps you can arrange the cranes so as to maximise coverage of the oil rig.
5 Finally, paint the quarters.

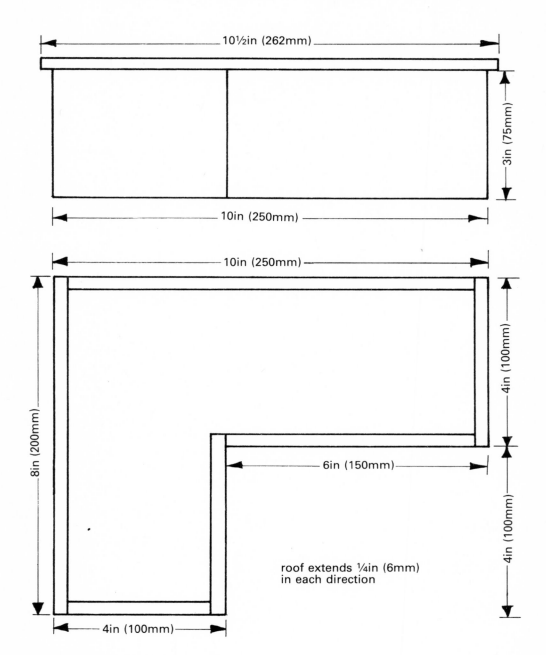

10½in (262mm)

3in (75mm)

10in (250mm)

10in (250mm)

4in (100mm)

8in (200mm)

6in (150mm)

4in (100mm)

roof extends ¼in (6mm)
in each direction

4in (100mm)

Fig 9 Side and plan view of crew quarters

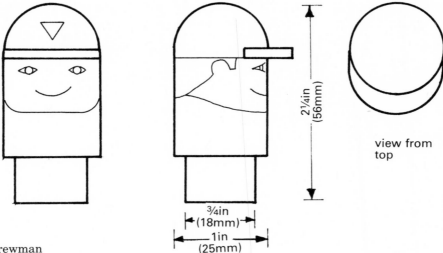

Fig 10 Crewman

view from
top

2¼in
(56mm)

¾in
(18mm)

1in
(25mm)

Crewmen
The crewmen are made from ¾in (18mm) and 1in (25mm) dowel.

1 Cut the two pieces to size (fig 10).
2 Locate the centre on the 1in (25mm) dowel and using a drill (see How To Do It, page 9) turn the top of the head until round.
3 Cut a thin piece of dowel for the peak of the hardhat and cut it in half. Cut a notch in the 1in (25mm) dowel using the fretsaw and glue the peak in place.
4 Fit the ¾in (18mm) dowel to the 1in (25mm) dowel.
5 Undercoat and paint them.

Derrick
1 Cut out the four outline shapes of the derrick (fig 11).
2 Nail them together through a couple of the waste triangular pieces and then cut out all the triangles in the four pieces at the same time. This cuts down the number of times you need to refit the blade. However, because all four sides are the same size, two of the sides of the derrick will be 4½in (112mm) along the bottom while the other two will be 5in (127mm) due to the thickness of the wood.
3 The top of the derrick is made from ½in (12mm) and ¾in (18mm) ply laminated together (see fig 11). Drill a hole through these pieces for the ⅜in (9mm) dowel of the drill handle.

4 Paint the derrick before assembling since painting the inside would otherwise be difficult.
5 Glue and nail the sides and top of the derrick together.
6 Make the drill handle (fig 11).
7 Cut 10in (254mm) lengths of ⅜in (9mm) dowel for the pipes making a half joint in both ends so that the pipes can be joined together. Drill a ⅛in (4mm) hole through these joints so that they can be linked with a piece of ⅛in (4mm) dowel (fig 11).

Helicopter Landing Pad
Cut this hexagon with an 8in (203mm) diameter from ½in (12mm) ply, drill a ⅜in (9mm) hole in the bottom and paint.

Platform/Box
The platform acts as a storage box for all the other parts of the toy. The legs I used are 6in (150mm) ready made legs that are sold complete with metal fixing plates from most DIY shops. When the toy is not in use the legs unscrew and can be stored inside the box.

1 Cut the top from ¼in (6mm) birch ply and the bottom and sides from ½in (12mm) birch ply (fig 12).
2 Decide where you want the derrick, crew's quarters, helicopter landing pad and cranes to be situated on the rig. Mark the centre of the derrick and either drill

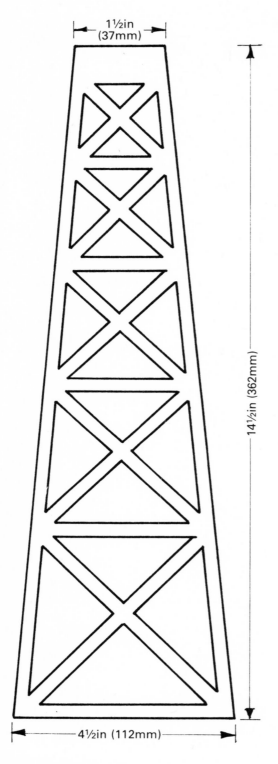

1½in
(37mm)

14½in (362mm)

4½in (112mm)

Fig 11a Oil rig derrick

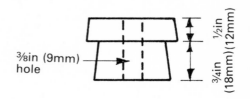

⅜in (9mm)
hole

½in
(12mm)

¾in
(18mm)

Fig 11b Top of derrick

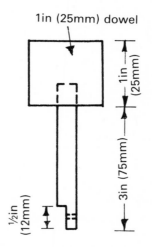

1in (25mm) dowel

1in
(25mm)

3in (75mm)

½in
(12mm)

Fig 11c Handle for turning drill

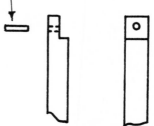

⅛in (4mm) dowel as pin joining pipes

Fig 11d Pin joints for joining pipes

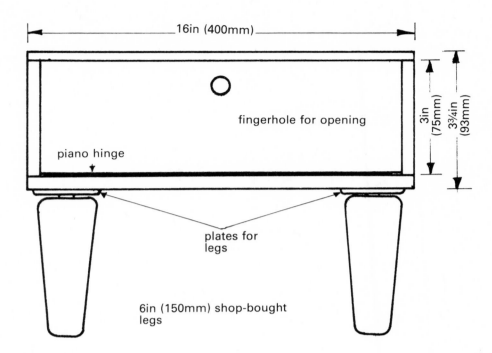

Fig 12 Oil rig platform/box

or cut a large hole through the top and bottom of the platform for the oil drill to pass through.

3 Drill ⅜in (9mm) holes in the top for the dowels to hold the crane and the helicopter pad in place.

4 Glue and nail the three sides, the top and the bottom together.

5 The fourth side is the access to the storage area. Drill or cut a finger hole for pulling the door open.

6 Fit the door in place using a length of piano hinge. I made the door a tight fit and did not need a fastener but if you like, use a magnetic catch.

7 Paint the platform. I used a simple criss-cross pattern for the sides; you may want to add more detail.

8 Fit the leg plates.

Supply Ship

1 It is a good idea to cut out the two bottom layers from ½in (12mm) ply at the same time to ensure a perfect match (fig 13).

2 Cut out the holds from the second layer (see How To Do It, page 7) and glue this layer to the bottom layer.

3 Cut out the top pieces for the stern and the bows and glue in place.

4 Make the superstructure from three pieces of ½in (12mm) ply (fig 13) glued together.

5 Drill ⅜in (9mm) holes for the two masts.

6 Cut the two masts from ⅜in (9mm) dowel. Drill a ⅛in (4mm) hole for the ⅛in (4mm) dowel crosspiece and fit them in place.

7 Cut the funnel from 1in (25mm) dowel.

8 Cut out the cargo containers from either ¾in (18mm) ply or ½in (12mm) and ¼in (6mm) ply laminated together. Drill a ⅛in (4mm) hole in each end for the crane hooks (fig 13).

9 Paint the funnel, superstructure and ship before assembling any further.

10 Nail through the bottom of the superstructure into the funnel and then glue the superstructure in place.

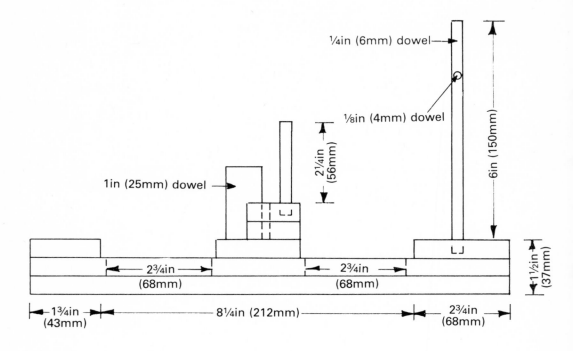

¼in (6mm) dowel

⅛in (4mm) dowel

1in (25mm) dowel

2¼in (56mm)

6in (150mm)

2¾in (68mm)

2¾in (68mm)

1½in (37mm)

1¾in (43mm)

8¼in (212mm)

2¾in (68mm)

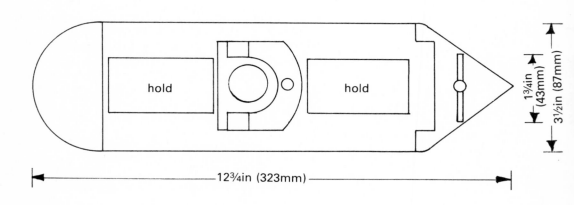

hold

hold

1¾in (43mm)

3½in (87mm)

12¾in (323mm)

holes for crane hooks

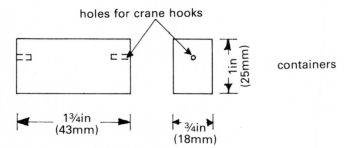

1in (25mm)

containers

1¾in (43mm)

¾in (18mm)

Fig 13 Oil rig supply ship construction and containers

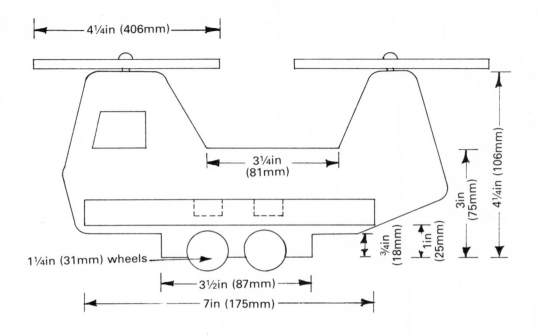

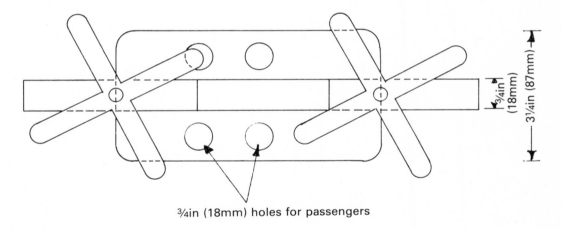

¾in (18mm) holes for passengers

Fig 14 Helicopter side and plan views

Helicopter
1 Cut out the shape of the helicopter from ¾in (18mm) ply (or use ¼in (6mm) and ½in (12mm) ply laminated together) (see How To Do It, page 7).
2 Cut out the window (fig 14) and the opening for the joint which holds the passengers' seats (fig 15) (see How To Do It, page 7). Drill holes for the axles.

3 Cut out the holes for the passengers.
4 Fit one side of the passenger seats. If you have made one joint a bit loose then nail through the helicopter body into the seat using the opposite seat to cover the nail. The second seat needs to be a better fit as you will not be able to nail it.
5 Make the wheels (see How To Do It, page 9).

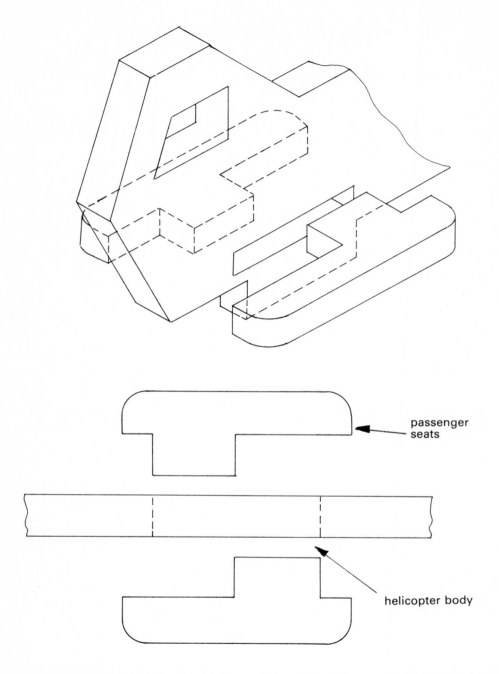

Fig 15 Method for fixing passenger seats in the helicopter

passenger seats

helicopter body

6 Cut out the rotor blades from ¼in (6mm) ply and drill a hole through the centre for the fixing screw.

7 Paint the helicopter, blades and wheels and then assemble.

This completes all the parts for the oil rig and it can now be played with indoors, outdoors or even in a paddling pool.

DOWN THE CHIMNEY

(shown in colour on page 52)

The original idea for this toy was to have Father Christmas dropping 'presents' down the chimney with his reindeer and sleigh parked around the back. The sleigh was going to be a container to hold the balls. I was also going to have snow on the roof with footprints leading to the chimney. But when 'push came to shove' I got fed up with it and the toy seemed good enough as it was. So, here is a challenge for you to take it further than I did. You can use the method for making the chess set pieces (page 47) to make the Father Christmas, and perhaps the methods used

for making the Cinderella coach and horses (page 27) to make the sleigh.

1 Cut out the 20×13×¼in (508×330× 6mm) back, the 17×13½×¼in (432× 342×6mm) front and the 20×1¾×¼in (508×44×6mm) sides from ply (fig 1 and 2).

2 Fit the 1¾in (44mm) wide chutes. It doesn't really matter how they are positioned (fig 3) as long as you note that one end is tight against the side wall of the house whilst the other has a gap for the ball to fall down. Also remember that the

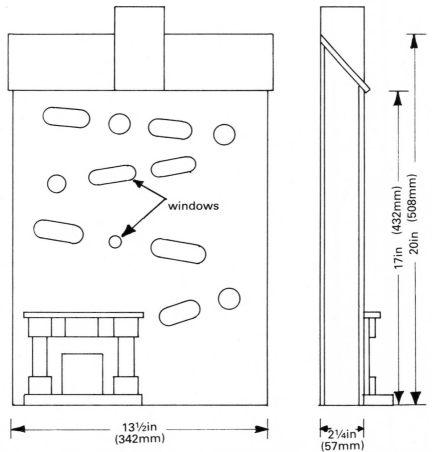

windows

17in (432mm)

20in (508mm)

13½in
(342mm)

2¼in
(57mm)

Fig 1 Wall showing position of windows and fireplace

Fig 2 Side view of wall showing the depth

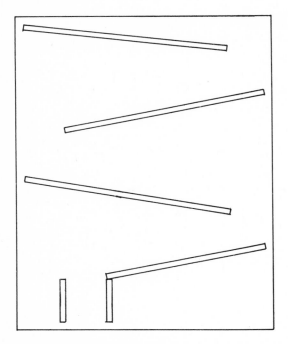

Fig 3 Arrangement of chutes inside the walls

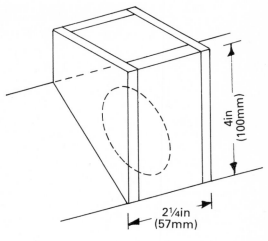

Fig 5 Chimney showing hole in the roof

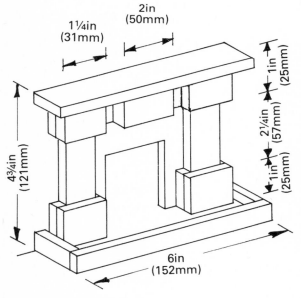

Fig 4 Fireplace construction

ball gathers momentum as it travels so it is advisable to make the lower slopes 'slower'. The upright pieces ensure that the ball comes out of the fireplace.

3 Cut out the windows smaller than the ball size, so that the path of the ball can be followed (fig 1).

4 Cut out a roof giving it a ¼in (6mm) overhang at each edge and cut a hole for the ball to pass through (fig 5).

5 Make up the chimney (fig 5) and fit it in place on the roof. Then fit the roof in place.

6 Make up the fireplace and hearth (fig 6) from small pieces of ¼in (6mm) ply.

7 Paint the house.

8 It is probably easier to buy a ball, but it needs to be wooden so that it will make a nice noise as it rolls down through the house. In every shop I have ever been into to try and buy wooden balls, the shop assistant has asked me what I want them for – even if they didn't stock them! If they ask *you*, tell them you are making a rocking horse!

If you can't buy a 1¼in (32mm) or 1½in (38mm) wooden ball, use the method described for making the heads for Tweedledee and Tweedledum (page 54). I did this, and although one end of the ball is a little bit flat where the screw fits for turning, the ball rolls perfectly well down through the house.

ALICE IN WONDERLAND CHESS SET

(shown in colour on page 51)

This is my favourite toy of the book, not because I am a chess fanatic but because it looks effective and is extremely simple to make. Over the years I had thought of several themes for chess sets but had never actually started one. I had read 'Alice' as a child and thought it a good story, but more recently I kept coming across references to 'Alice's Adventures in Wonderland' and 'Alice through the Looking Glass' by Lewis Carroll in mathematics, physics and biology textbooks, which implied that there was more to the book than I had thought. Since my daughter had both copies, I reread them and realised it was the type of book that can be read on two levels; children's and adults'. The idea of making a chess set based on an Alice theme was far more persistent than the others, the one remaining problem was whether it would be too difficult to make or too tedious with all those pawns. I decided to start with the piece which I thought would be the most difficult, 'The Mad Hatter'. If it didn't work out I would only have wasted a few inches of wood, but if the hardest piece turned out well, the rest would follow. As it happened, none of the pieces was in any way difficult to construct. It is the paintwork that makes them look so good – do use good brushes (see How To Do It, page 8). When making the board remember that the widest part of some pieces is not the base (eg Cheshire Cat) and so the squares need to be wider.

You will probably notice that I have made eight different characters plus the pawns. This is because I didn't want to make, say, four Hatters or four Cheshire Cats when there is such a wealth of characters to choose from. Obviously, when using the set, the players will have to agree which characters represent which pieces. So let's start with the 'Mad Hatter' which probably looks the most difficult and is essential to the set anyway.

Mad Hatter

1 Start with the hat. In fig 1 you can see that the hat is made from four layers of ½in (12mm) ply and one layer of ⅛in (4mm) ply for the brim. Draw the circles for the hat on the ply and mark the centres for the screw for turning (see How To Do It, page 9). Cut out the four pieces.

2 Glue and nail the three ½in (12mm) pieces together and turn them using rough sandpaper until you get a shape similar to the drawing.

3 Since the end grain of the ply will be exposed on all the pieces, wood filler is essential for this toy (see How To Do It, page 8). Apply it to the hat now. When it is dry turn it against medium sandpaper and finally against fine sandpaper.

4 Turn the brim in the same way and attach it to the hat.

5 Now the bit that *looks* hard. Cut out the pieces marked a, b and c in figs 1 and 2. These make up the forehead and the nose. Using the fretsaw, cut the curl of hair at each side of the face on the three pieces.

6 Glue b and c together and cut the triangular waste pieces from the nose as in the side view (fig 1). Then do the same for the full face view.

7 Sand the nose, rounding it until it becomes a nice 'nose' shape.

8 Glue a to b and c.

9 Cut out the layer for the mouth and cut the hair curls in the same way. Glue this layer in place.

10 The two bottom layers are the shoulder and the neck which are cut from ¼in (6mm) and ½in (12mm) ply the same shape as 'a', but the sides are cut off a little.

11 The bow tie is made from ⅛ (4mm) ply and glued in place.

12 The price tag is either ⅛in (4mm) or 1/16in (2mm) ply glued in place.

13 The final step for each chess piece is to fill any blemishes, sand and paint it.

Now that you have seen how easy the

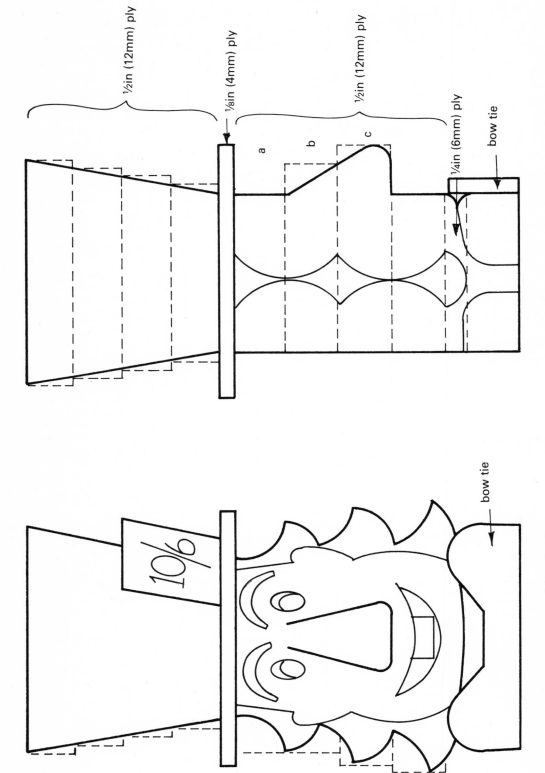

Fig 1 Mad Hatter construction and face detail

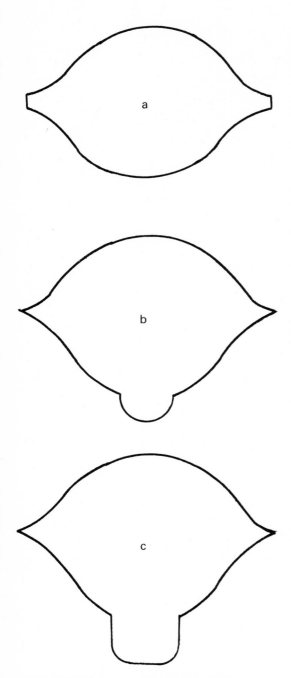

Fig 2 Mad Hatter, shapes of head pieces from above

'hardest' piece is, it is a good idea to try the most numerous piece – the pawn. Thankfully there is very little to do since most of the pawn consists of a few lengths of dowelling. A drill stand would have been a great help for this toy; I drilled a few holes in the wrong places before getting them all correct.

Pawn

1 For the head cut a piece of 1in (25mm) dowel 1⅛in (28mm) long, locate the centre and insert the screw for turning and turn the head until round (fig 3a). I cut a curved notch in the underside of the head of my first pawn (see fig 3b). But by the time I had finished the last one I wished I hadn't bothered, and to be honest it doesn't improve the appearance very much – so please yourself.

2 Cut the body from ¾in (18mm) dowel and drill a ¼in (6mm) hole through the centre.

3 Cut the 'legs', 'neck' etc in one length about 4in (100mm) long and push it through the hole in the body.

4 Cut the notches for the playing cards.

5 For the hands drill a hole off centre in the end of a length of ¾in (18mm) dowel and glue a piece of ¼in (6mm) dowel into it for the arms (see figs 3b and c). Using the fretsaw cut the hands to shape. It is easier working in this order as you can then hold the length of ¾in (18mm) dowel while you cut rather than trying to drill into a very small piece of wood.

6 Drill the arm holes in the body and glue the arms in place adjusting them until they actually hold the playing card (fig 3c).

7 Cut out the feet, drill a ¼in (6mm) hole for the legs and glue them in place.

8 Glue on the head.

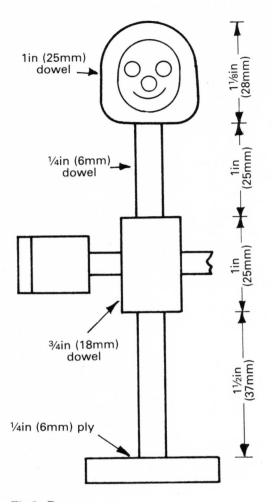

1in (25mm)
dowel →

¼in (6mm)
dowel →

¾in (18mm)
dowel

¼in (6mm) ply

1⅛in (28mm)

1in (25mm)

1in (25mm)

1½in (37mm)

Fig 3a Pawn

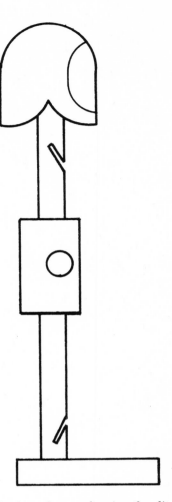

Fig 3b Side view of pawn showing the slits for the playing cards

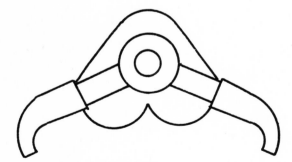

Fig 3c Top view of pawn showing the position of the hands to hold the card

Alice in Wonderland Chess Set (page 47)

50

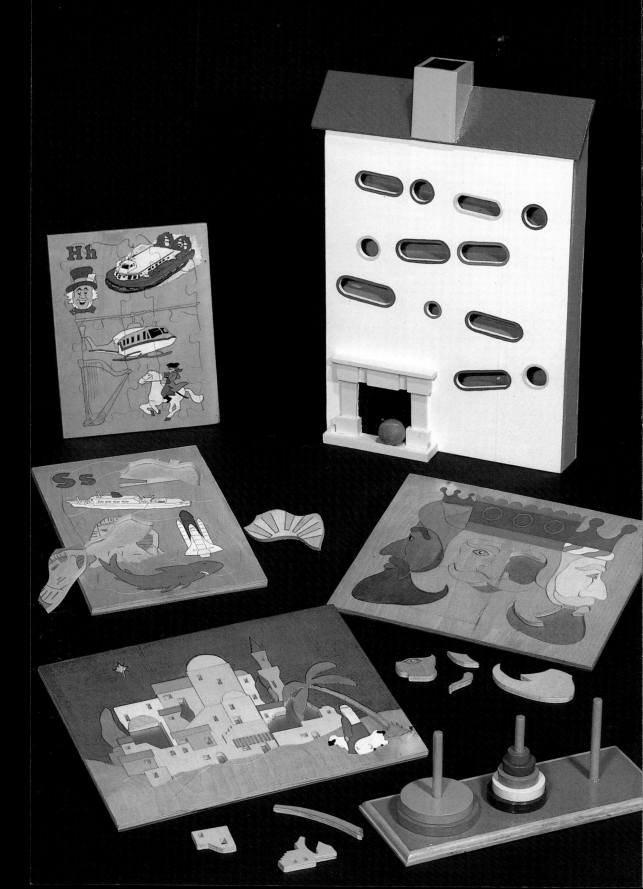

Humpty Dumpty

This is a favourite character of mine because in the story Humpty pays his words extra so that they mean exactly what *he* wants them to mean. I have done the same, so if you think I have made a mistake, it's just that I've paid some words extra to mean something else. Neat isn't it?

1 Cut out the rings (fig 4a).
2 Turn the rings (see How To Do It, page 9).
3 Cut out the hands from ¼in (6mm) ply (fig 4b) and the feet from ½in (12mm) ply (fig 4c). Cut a notch for the heel of the boot and round the toe with sandpaper. You will find it easier to drill the holes for the arms and legs prior to cutting out the hands and feet.
4 Drill holes for the arms and legs. This is the most difficult part, unless you have a drill stand as drilling into a curved surface is not easy. I used my smallest drill bit to drill pilot holes and then used progressively larger bits until I reached ¼in (6mm). Doing it this way I didn't have any problems.
5 Cut the wall from two pieces of ½in (12mm) ply and glue Humpty in place (fig 4a).

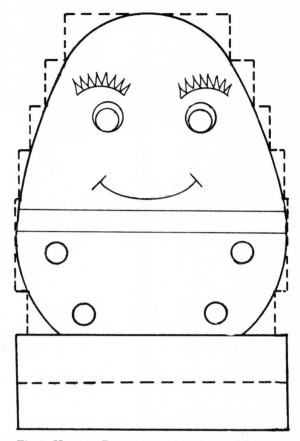

Fig 4a Humpty Dumpty construction and face detail

¼in (6mm) ply

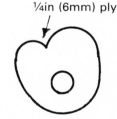

Fig 4b Humpty's hands

¼in (6mm) dowel

½in (12mm) ply

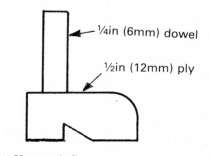

Alphabet Puzzles (page 14); Down the Chimney (page 45); Christmas Jigsaw Puzzles (page 18); Tower of Hanoi Puzzle (page 21)

Fig 4c Humpty's feet

53

Tweedledee and Tweedledum

1 Make the body and head separately. Make the head from two pieces of ½in (12mm) ply and one piece of ¼in (6mm) ply (fig 5a).
2 Turn the five pieces of the body first to get the correct shape and then add the two pieces of the legs and turn them altogether.
3 Cut out the feet (fig 5b), rounding the toes with sandpaper.
4 Glue on the head and feet.

White Rabbit

1 Make the top of the head from two pieces of ½in (12mm) ply (fig 6).
2 Make the cheeks from three pieces of ½in (12mm) ply.
3 Make the neck from one piece of ½in (12mm) ply.
4 With a file or sandpaper, flatten one side of a piece of ⅜in (9mm) dowel for one of the ears and round one end. Cut the other ear in the middle at an angle and glue it back together to give the appearance of a floppy ear. This must be done before flattening the side of the dowel.
5 Following the procedure used in Humpty Dumpty drill holes for the ears.
6 Glue the top of the head, cheeks and neck together.
7 Cut out the shoulders from ½in (12mm) and ¼in (6mm) ply, round them off and glue to the neck.

Cheshire Cat

When I play with the set I make the rule that the Cheshire Cat can disappear from the board but still guards the same squares. You can always tell when he is coming back by the smile on the player's face as his opponent crosses the Cat's path.

1 Turn the body and the head separately (fig 7).
2 You now need to take a slice off the body to fit the head on. Draw around the base of the head on to a piece of cardboard and cut out the centre of the circle; this will then act as a template, fitting over the body to give you a sawing guide.
3 Drill holes for the ears and nose as for Humpty Dumpty.

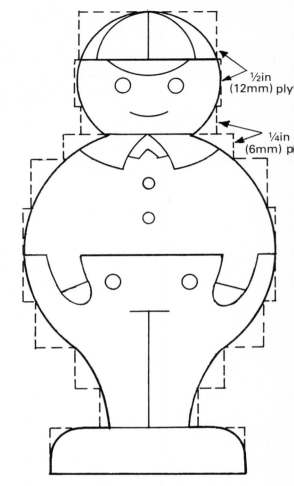

Fig 5a Tweedledee and Tweedledum construction and detail

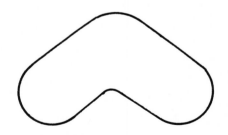

Fig 5b Shape for their feet

4 Flatten the front of the ears after they have been glued in place (fig 7).
5 Round the end of a piece of ¼in (6mm) dowel and glue it in place for the nose.
6 Glue the head to the body.

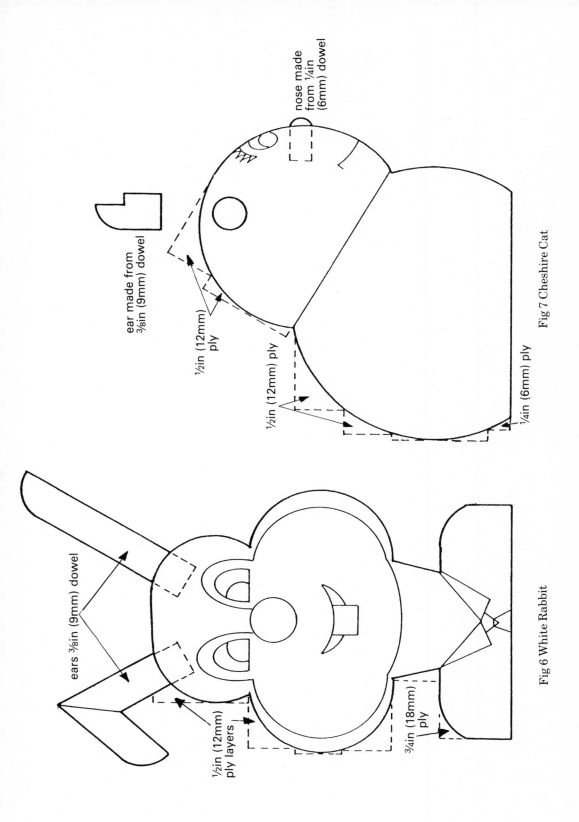

nose made from ¼in (6mm) dowel

ear made from ⅜in (9mm) dowel

½in (12mm) ply

½in (12mm) ply

½in (12mm) ply

¼in (6mm) ply

Fig 7 Cheshire Cat

ears ⅜in (9mm) dowel

½in (12mm) ply layers

¾in (18mm) ply

Fig 6 White Rabbit

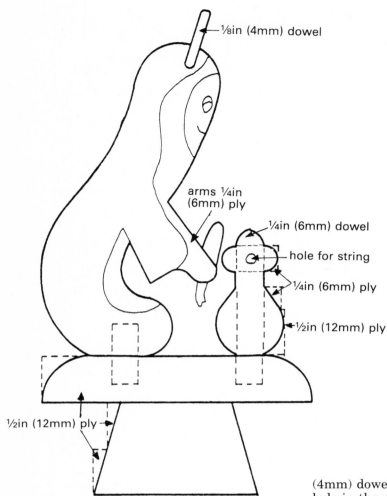

⅛in (4mm) dowel

arms ¼in (6mm) ply

¼in (6mm) dowel

hole for string

¼in (6mm) ply

½in (12mm) ply

½in (12mm) ply

Fig 8a Caterpillar with pipe

½in (12mm) ply

¼in (6mm) ply

Fig 8b Caterpillar front view

Caterpillar
1 Make the mushroom in two pieces, the cap and the stem (fig 8a).
2 Cut out the side shapes (fig 8b) of the caterpillar from a piece of ½in (12mm) ply and two pieces of ¼in (6mm) ply. The ¼in (6mm) ply contains the arms, the central ½in (12mm) piece does not. To make it more interesting have one arm pointing down and perhaps the other pointing forwards.
3 Glue these three pieces together and sand the body until it is rounded. I used a sanding disc attachment on my drill.
4 Drill ⅛in (4mm) holes for the ⅛in

(4mm) dowel antennae and a ¼in (6mm) hole in the caterpillar and the mushroom to join them together with ¼in (6mm) dowel.
5 Drill a small hole for the string in the edge of ¼in (6mm) ply and then cut the hookah pipe from the ply.
6 The hookah jar is made from a length of ¼in (6mm) dowel pushed through circular pieces of ½in (12mm) and ¼in (6mm) ply. The bottom of the ¼in (6mm) dowel is inserted in the drill bit and turned in order to round the hookah jar.
7 Drill a small hole in the jar for the string and a ¼in (6mm) hole in the mushroom for the jar.
8 Put a blob of glue in both the string holes and then poke one end of the string into the jar and the other end into the pipe.

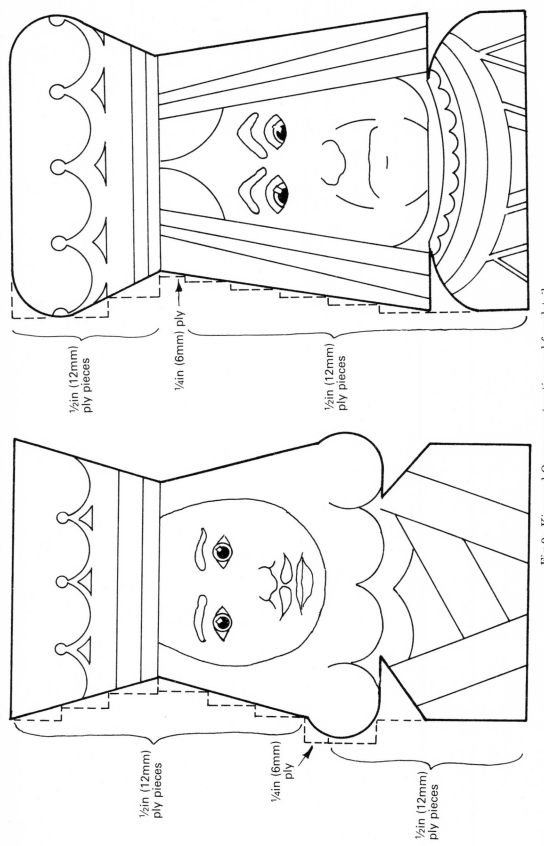

½in (12mm) ply pieces

¼in (6mm) ply

½in (12mm) ply pieces

½in (12mm) ply pieces

¼in (6mm) ply

½in (12mm) ply pieces

Fig 9a King and Queen construction and face detail

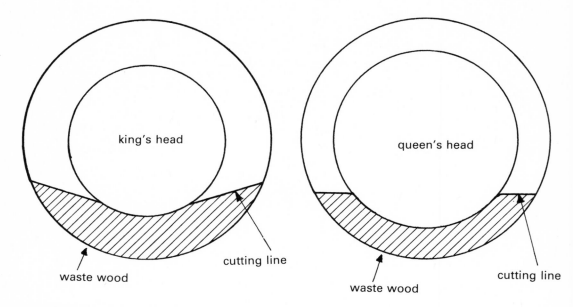

Fig 9b Plans for shape of King and Queen's heads, without crowns

King and Queen
These two pieces are very similar in construction so I'll describe them together.

1 Make the crowns separately (fig 9a).
2 For the face you may find it easier if you screw the rings together while you turn them rather than glueing them. Thus you can unscrew them in order to cut the front of the face (fig 9b) in single layers instead of six layers at once. If you would prefer to cut them all at once then I recommend that you use a coping saw in place of the fretsaw.
3 Cut out the shoulders.
4 Glue the shoulders and crown to the head.

Chess Board
This set was for children to play with so I made a simple board from ¼in (6mm) ply which wouldn't be too heavy for them to carry around. The squares are 3¼in (82mm) (make sure your pieces will fit in this size square) and I allowed a ⅝in (16mm) border.

1 Cut the board to size.
2 Varnish the board with clear varnish.
3 Mark out the squares.
4 Mask off the plain squares with adhesive tape and stain the 'black' squares. I used walnut stain. When the adhesive tape is removed it leaves clean crisp lines. Varnish the whole board and paint the White Rabbit on to it (fig 10). When I had finished my daughter Natasha asked 'Where's Alice?'. I told her she could be Alice when she played with it; if you have a son you could be in trouble.

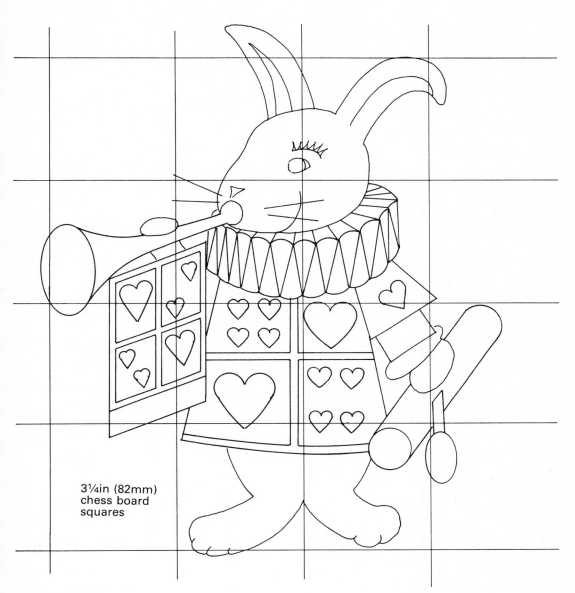

3¼in (82mm)
chess board
squares

Fig 10 Chessboard motif

RIDING SCHOOL

(shown in colour on page 88)

This is a very simple toy made more elaborate by the addition of a Land Rover and horse trailer. I used ⅜in (9mm) birch ply for the stables and horse trailer but only ¼in (6mm) ply for the Land Rover and figures. I have drawn the plans accordingly. The only reason I used ¼in (6mm) ply for the Land Rover was that I made it before the riding school and at the time I didn't have any ⅜in (9mm) ply, so I just used what I had. Since the Land Rover is the toy out of this set which will probably get the roughest treatment, the ¼in (6mm) ply would clearly be strong enough for the horse trailer and stables. However, it would make purchasing easier to use only one thickness – my own preference is ⅜in (9mm). Similarly I have used plastic wheels on the Land Rover and wooden ones on the horse trailer, merely to illustrate the difference – I prefer the plastic ones.

Stables

1 Cut out the two 14×5in (356×127mm) pieces of ⅜in (9mm) birch ply for the front and back (fig 1).

2 Mark out the stable doors and window and cut them out (see How To Do It, page 7).

3 Cut out the two gable ends (fig 2) and cut out the office door and window in only one end.

4 Cut and fit the doors – I used short strips of piano hinge although other hinges would be just as suitable.

5 Glue and nail the back and front to the sides.

6 Fix the two 6¼×5in (158×125mm) internal walls.

7 Glue and nail the front of the roof in place.

8 The rear roof is removable so a strip of wood needs to be glued and nailed to each end of the roof (fig 2) to hold it loosely in place.

9 For the 20×14in (508×356mm) base I

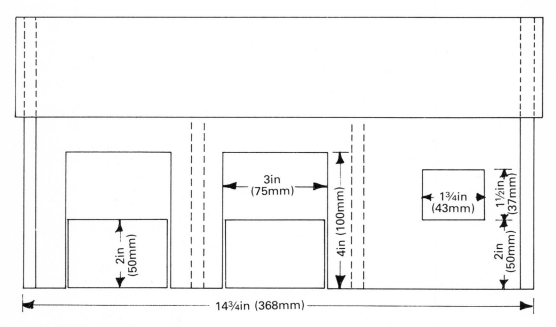

Fig 1 Front and back shape of stable block

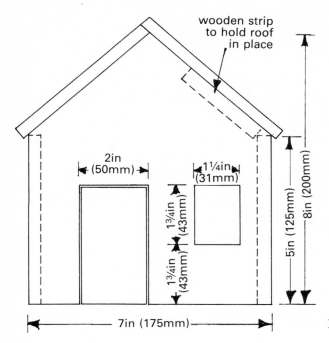

wooden strip
to hold roof
in place

2in
(50mm)

1¼in
(31mm)

1¾in
(43mm)

1¾in
(43mm)

5in (125mm)

8in (200mm)

7in (175mm)

Fig 2 Side view of stables with door

would normally use either ⅛in (4mm) hardboard or ply, but I had been given some scrap ⅜in (9mm) chipboard so I used that.

10 Paint the stables and base and then glue and nail the base to the stables.

11 The cart wheels leaning against the stable walls are like those on the Cinderella Coach and are only for decoration.

Fences

I have included one drawing (fig 3) for a fence, for additional fences use pieces of dowelling balanced on small blocks of wood. The illustrated fence is made from ¼in (6mm) ply with a ½×½in (12× 12mm) post each side of the gate. Glue and nail a small base to each post and then glue and nail the post to the gate.

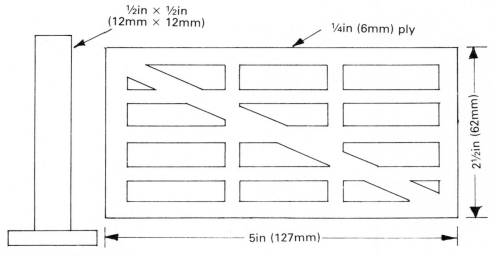

½in × ½in
(12mm × 12mm)

¼in (6mm) ply

2½in (62mm)

5in (127mm)

Fig 3 Fence for riding school

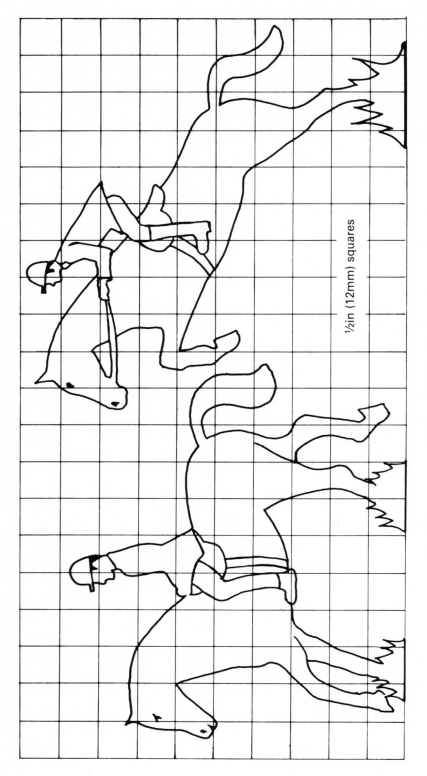

½in (12mm) squares

Fig 4 Horses with riders

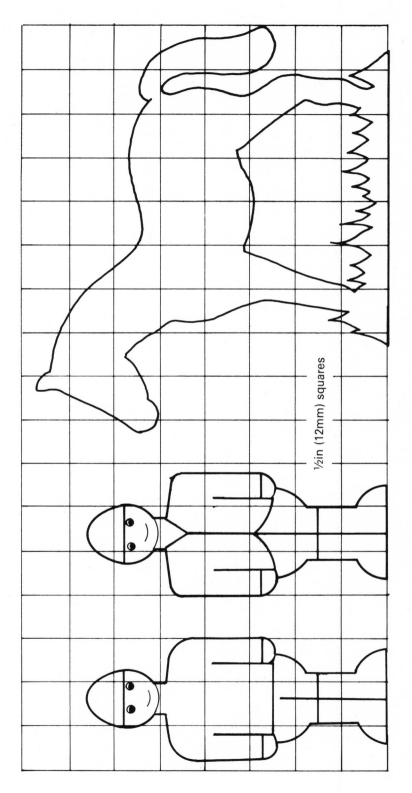

½in (12mm) squares

Fig 5 Horse and riders

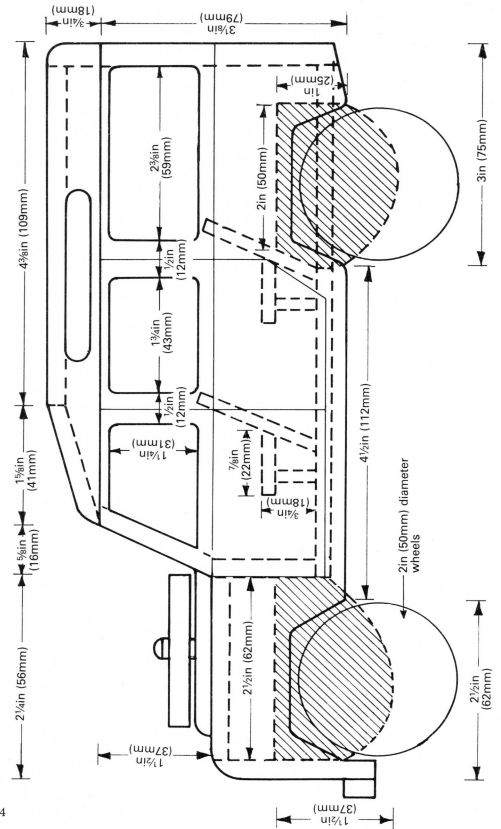

Fig 6 Land Rover, side view

64

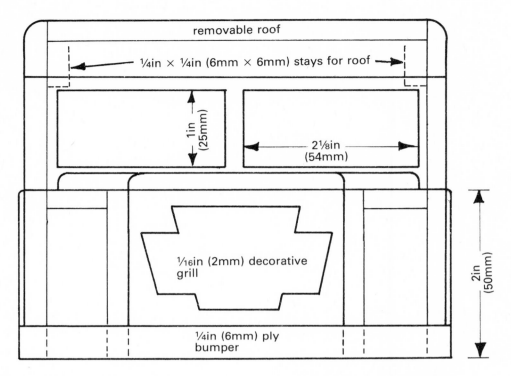

Fig 7 (above) Front of Land Rover   Fig 8 (below) Back of Land Rover

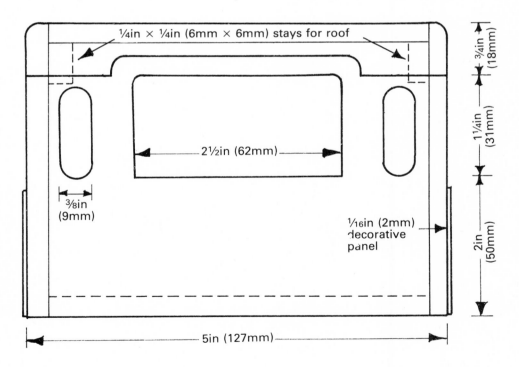

Riding School Figures

1 Cut the shapes (figs 4 and 5) out of ¼in (6mm) birch ply at the same time cutting small bases for them.
2 Glue and nail the bases to the figures.
3 Paint the figures.

Fig 9 Land Rover hood

Land Rover

One of my earliest jobs was working on a pipeline which ran across country and in order to travel the site, off-road vehicles were required. Consequently one of the first vehicles I drove was a Land Rover, so I suppose I have a bit of a soft spot for them.

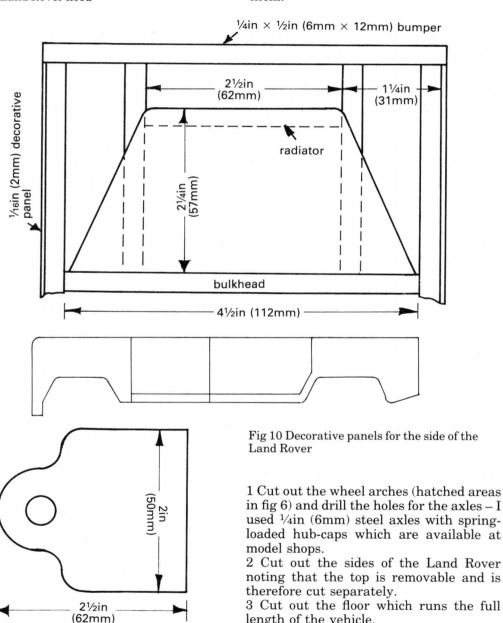

Fig 10 Decorative panels for the side of the Land Rover

Fig 11 Land Rover coupling

1 Cut out the wheel arches (hatched areas in fig 6) and drill the holes for the axles – I used ¼in (6mm) steel axles with spring-loaded hub-caps which are available at model shops.
2 Cut out the sides of the Land Rover noting that the top is removable and is therefore cut separately.
3 Cut out the floor which runs the full length of the vehicle.
4 Cut out the back (fig 8) and the windscreen.

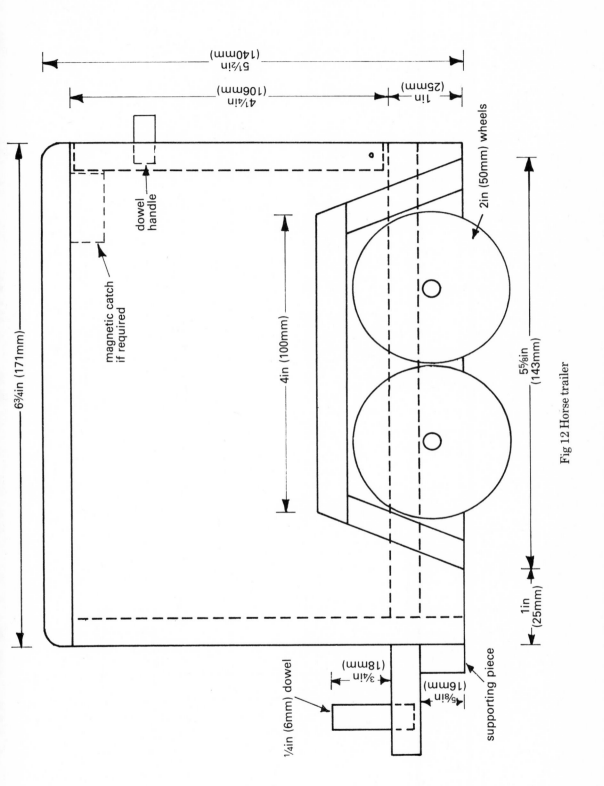

Fig 12 Horse trailer

5 Cut out all the windows (see How To Do It, page 7).

6 Glue the wheel arches to the inside of the sides.

7 Fit the sides to the floor and fit the windscreen to the sides.

8 Make the bench seats and fit in place. The rear wheel-arch acts as a support for the back seat. Nail through the sides into the seats. I have a long-handled artist's brush which makes painting much easier. If you haven't, it might be a good idea to paint the interior of the vehicle and the seats before fitting them.

9 Fit the bulkhead between the engine and passenger compartments.

10 Make the wings and engine compartment (figs 7 and 9).

11 Make the hood from ⅛in (4mm) ply (fig 9).

12 Cut out the pieces for the roof and fit them together (figs 6, 7 and 8) including some ¼×¼in (6×6mm) stays to hold the roof in place.

Castle (page 108); St George and the Dragon (page 125); Medieval Catapult (page 120)

13 Fit the bumper.

14 Fit the decorative panels down the sides (fig 10) and the radiator grill. The decorative grill is exactly the same shape as the lower half of the vehicle but is cut into five separate pieces (fig 6). Make sure that the joins are evident as this is the point of these panels.

15 If you are going to make the horse trailer then cut out and fit the coupling (fig 11).

16 Paint it and finally fit the wheels. Use either ready made wheels or make your own (see How To Do It, page 9).

Horse Trailer

1 Cut out the sides, front and roof (figs 12 and 13) and drill holes in the sides for the axles.

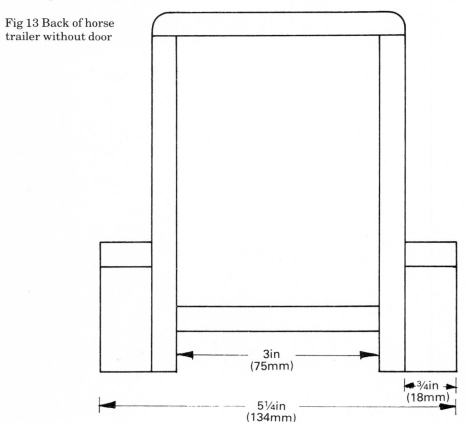

Fig 13 Back of horse trailer without door

3in
(75mm)

¾in
(18mm)

5¼in
(134mm)

1 Doll's Kitchen (page 89); 2 Clown (page 134); 3 Panda Bookshelf (page 11); 4 Doll's Music Box Piano (page 23); 5 Rocking Parrot (page 11); 6 Gymnast (page 132); 7 Toddler's Merry-go-round (page 101); 8 Chromatrope (page 130); 9 Thaumatrope (page 131)

2 Cut out the door/ramp and drill a small hole near the bottom (fig 12) on each long edge. This will be part of a home-made hinge.

3 Tap a panel pin through each of the sides – the hole in the door/ramp will fit over it and will complete the hinge.

4 Cut out, glue and nail the mud guards to the sides of the horse trailer.

5 Glue and nail the front and one side to the floor.

6 Fit the door/ramp in position on the panel pin and check that the door opens and closes properly and then fit the other side.

7 I made the door a tight fit but if you prefer, add a magnetic cabinet catch (fig 12). A small piece of dowel acts as a handle.

8 Cut out the coupling (fig 14) and fit the ¼in (6mm) dowel in place. Glue and nail the coupling to the ⅝in (16mm) supporting piece (fig 12) and then glue and nail both to the horse trailer.

9 Paint the horse trailer and fit either the plastic or wooden wheels.

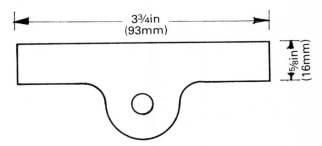

Fig 14 Coupling for horse trailer

STACKING BEEFEATER

(shown in colour on page 34)

I completed the woodworking part of this toy in about two hours and it looked very effective in the plain wood but the colours really brought out the best. I think a fine brush is essential for painting the detail (see How To Do It, page 8). In fig 1 I have tried to give some indication of the details without cluttering up the drawing which would make it difficult to read. The basic colour is bright red with black bands on a yellow (gold) background. There are red, white and blue rosettes on his hat, shoes, the side of his legs and on his lance. I was unable to find a decent photograph of a real beefeater, the best I found was in a pub on a bottle of gin – making a sketch on a beer mat is not an ideal method of research. If you want more authentic detail take a trip to London or better still, buy a bottle of gin!

The idea of the toy is to remove the pieces from the central pole, which is glued into the feet, mix them up and then replace them in the correct order; so far no one has been able to manage it at the first attempt. When I finally came to assemble it I thought I had painted one of the rings with the sash going the wrong way and I was none too pleased until I found I had got it upside down.

The amount of wood required for this toy is so small that a timber merchant will be able to let you have enough out of his off-cuts and it should therefore be very inexpensive. The method for turning rings etc, is described in How To Do It (page 9).

1 Start with the hat; this is 1in (25mm) thick, 2⅜in (59mm) in diameter tapering to 2in (50mm). When you have the correct shape and are satisfied that it is ready for painting, drill a ¼in (6mm) hole about ½in (12mm) deep into the underside of the hat. This will produce a tight fit and keep all the lower pieces in place.
2 The brim of the hat is 3in (75mm) in diameter and ¼in (6mm) thick.

3 The face is 1¼in (30mm) thick and made from a couple of ⅝in (15mm) thicknesses glued together. Round the bottom of the face with sandpaper.
4 The ruff is ½in (12mm) thick and 2⅝in (66mm) in diameter.
5 The shoulders and chest are ¾in (18mm) thick and 3in (75mm) in diameter. Turn the shoulders until they are slightly round (fig 1). Drill a ¼in (6mm) diameter hole in each side of the chest for the arms.
6 The stomach is ¾in (18mm) thick, 3in (75mm) in diameter tapering to 2½in (63mm).
7 The waist is ½in (12mm) thick and 2½in (63mm) in diameter.
8 The next three pieces make up the skirt of the coat and are all ¾in (18mm) thick and start at 2½in (63mm) in diameter increasing to 3¾in (93mm).
9 The legs consist of three pieces, ¾in (18mm) thick tapering from 2in (50mm) to ¾in (18mm) diameter.
10 The feet are ¾in (18mm) thick and shaped as in fig 2. Round the toes with sandpaper.
11 Drill a ¼in (6mm) hole in the feet for the ¼in (6mm) dowel central pole. Stack the rings to determine the length of the pole; it may be as well to cut the pole a little longer than you think you need and trim it later.
12 Drill a hole through the centre of each of the remaining pieces a little larger than the pole's diameter, say 5⁄16in (8mm) to make it easy to place the rings on the pole. Take care to drill the holes accurately, both centrally and vertically.
13 The arms are made from ¾in (18mm) dowel, 4in (100mm) long with ¼in (6mm) dowel pegs to fit them to the chest. Round the shoulders and hands with sandpaper as in fig 1. The right arm is hinged. To make the hinge, cut the joint as shown in the drawing. Either drill a ⅛in (3mm) hole through the complete joint and fit a piece of ⅛in (3mm) dowel, glueing it to

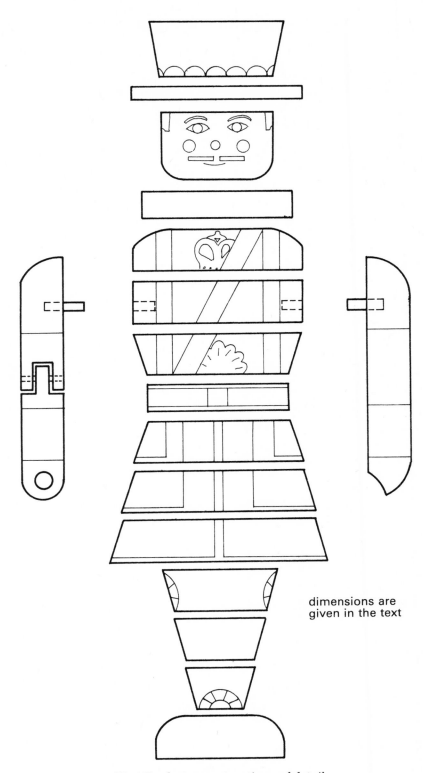

dimensions are
given in the text

Fig 1 Beefeater construction and detail

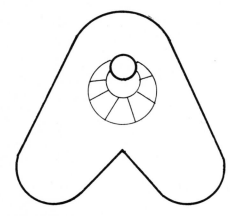

Fig 2 Beefeater's feet

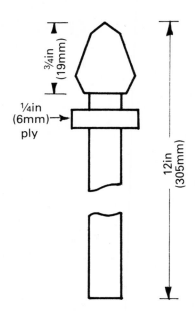

¾in (19mm)

¼in (6mm)→ ply

12in (305mm)

Fig 3 Beefeater's lance

the outer part of the joint (mortise), or drill a small hole through the inner part (tenon) of the joint and tap a small panel pin through one side of the mortise, through the hole in the tenon, and into the other side of the mortise. Whichever method you decide to use, it is far easier if you paint the joint before assembling it. Drill a ⁵⁄₁₆in (8mm) hole through the hand for the lance.

14 For the lance drill a ¼in (6mm) hole in a small piece of ¾in (18mm) thick timber, and in a piece of ¼in (6mm) ply. Then cut a circle around the hole in the ply for the rosette and glue it on the lance. Glue the ¾in (18mm) thick timber on the end of the ¼in (6mm) shaft of the lance and *then* cut the point (fig 3), otherwise it will be too small to hold safely whilst cutting it.

15 Finally paint the toy. A useful tip is to hold the rings by their edges and paint both sides, placing them on a length of dowel to paint the edges. This way you can paint them all in one go and there will not be a double layer of paint where you left off.

OLD-FASHIONED BUS

(shown in colour on page 87)

I was very conscious of the fact that this is a book for toy-making beginners as well as those who are experienced when I was doing the drawings for this bus. Drawings can become confusing if there are too many dimensions, but if there are too few it can be equally annoying for more obvious reasons. I think I have included more dimensions than are actually required, hopefully without making the drawings look complicated. This is the type of toy where the drawings may needlessly deter the beginner. So before getting down to details I'll describe how I actually made this toy. I didn't have any drawings but I knew the shape the bus was going to take, also that it was to have 4in (100mm) wheels and that the passengers were to be 5in (127mm) or 6in (152mm) dolls.

I started by placing the wheels on a piece of ⅜in (9mm) ply and moving them apart until they looked about right. I then marked the wheel arches directly on to the wood and gradually built up a picture of the whole side of the bus. At this point I lightly nailed this piece on to another piece of ⅜in (9mm) ply and cut them both out together. The important thing to note is that I had only drawn the outline at this point and had not even considered the windows. Some beginners make the mistake of using the intermediate measurements, say, the windows and window frames rather than the overall measurement. This may seem trivial as the sum of the intermediate measurements should equal the whole; but if your measurements are not quite accurate, a small error in marking out each of the windows could lead to a substantial difference in the overall size of the piece.

The next step is to cut out the front, back and bottom which are all the same width. This was now sufficient for me to be able to hold the pieces together with adhesive tape to get an overall impression of the toy and I suggest you do the same.

1 Mark out a side of the bus (fig 1) on ⅜in (9mm) birch ply; forget about the door and windows for the time being.

2 Using panel pins, lightly nail this side on to another piece of ⅜in (9mm) ply and cut the two sides out in one cut (a coping saw may be better than a fretsaw for this, see How To Do It, page 7).

3 Mark and cut out fig 2, back of bus.

4 Do the same for the top deck front and the drivers partition (figs 3 and 4).

5 Cut out the 25⅜in × 8½in (644mm × 216mm) bottom of the bus.

6 Mark out the windows on one side, pin the sides together again. Cut out the windows and drill the holes for the ¼in (6mm) steel axles.

7 Separate the two sides and cut out the door (shaded area fig 1), on one side only.

8 Cut out the door and openings in the back of the bus (fig 2), top deck front openings (fig 3), and the drivers partition windows (fig 4).

9 Cut out the reinforcing pieces for the front wheel arches (fig 5, hatched area) glue and nail them to the *inside* of the buses' side and drill the axle holes through these pieces.

10 Cut out the rear wheel arch reinforcing pieces. These are the same shape as the front except that they include the whole area inside the mudguard (fig 5), not just the hatched area. Glue and nail these pieces in place on the *outside* of the bus side pieces. Re-drill the axle holes.

11 Cut two chassis pieces (fig 6) from 2in × 1in (50mm × 25mm) softwood. I haven't included measurements on the drawing as the best way of marking them out is to place the side of the bus on top of the softwood, allowing the bus to cover ⅜in (9mm) of it, and the softwood to extend ⅜in (9mm) below the side of the bus, (hatched area in fig 6). These pieces give extra strength to the bus and also serve to hold up the floor. Glue and nail them to the sides of the bus and drill the axle holes through them.

75

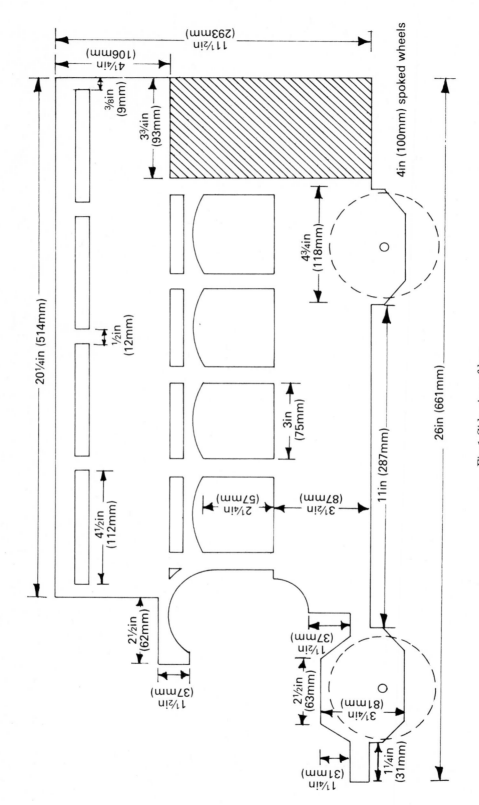

Fig 1 Side view of bus

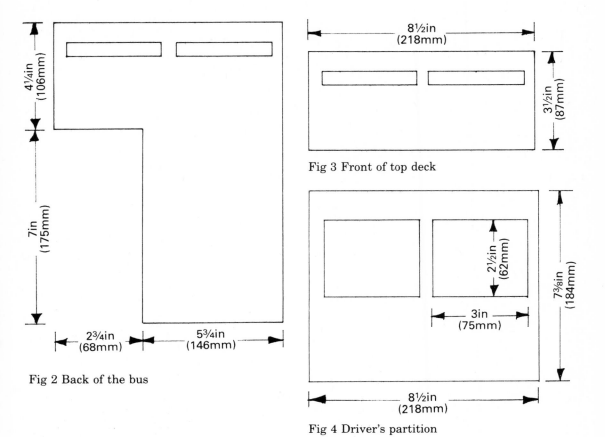

Fig 2 Back of the bus

Fig 3 Front of top deck

Fig 4 Driver's partition

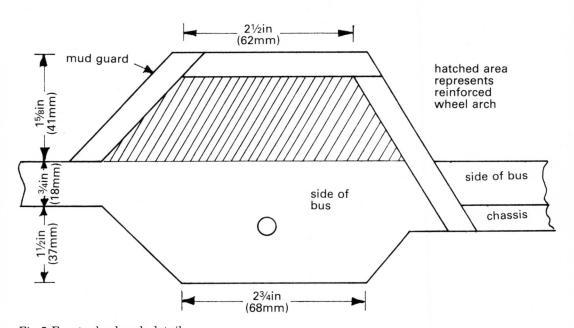

mud guard

hatched area
represents
reinforced
wheel arch

side of bus

side of
bus

chassis

Fig 5 Front wheel arch detail

cut from 2in × 1in (50mm × 25mm) softwood

Fig 6 Bus chassis

2in
(50mm)

½in
(12mm)

2in
(50mm)

⅞in
(22mm)

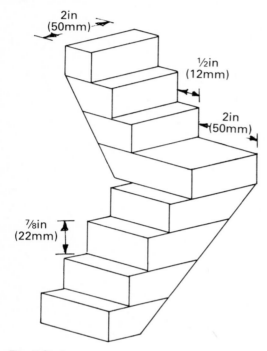

Fig 7 Staircase

1in (25mm)
1in (25mm)
1in (25mm)
¾in (18mm)

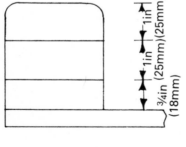

12 Now it is time to make a start on putting the bus together. Glue and nail the back to the side without the door. Glue and nail the front top deck to the same side. Glue and nail the floor in place.

13 Now that the floor is in, make the staircase as in fig 7, from the same 2×1in (50×25mm) softwood as the chassis. I used PAR (planed all round) and the finished size was ⅞in (22mm) as in the drawing. The actual height of the staircase is not critical but if your wood is exactly 1in (25mm), which is unlikely, you will gain 1in (25mm) over the eight stairs, so miss a stair. I covered the exposed edges of the staircase with ¼in (6mm) ply to act as a facia.

14 Glue and nail the stairs in place.

15 Make the seats using ⅜in (9mm) ply and 2×1in (50×25mm) softwood (fig 8), and fit them in place on the lower deck. I placed two wide seats sideways near the door and staircase and then three wide seats and three narrow seats, either side of the aisle, in a similar position to those on the upper deck (see fig 11).

16 Fit the driver's partition and the top deck front.

17 Make a seat for the driver similar to the passenger seats.

18 Make a steering wheel (fig 9) from ⅜in (9mm) ply and ¼in (6mm) dowel. Drill a hole in the floor and glue it in place.

stairwell

2¾in
(68mm)

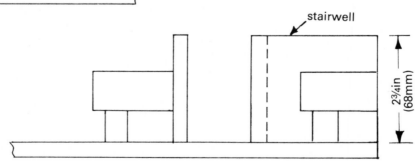

Fig 8 Front and side view of seats

Fig 9 Bus steering wheel

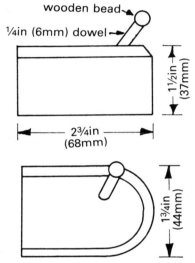

Fig 10 Bus gear box and gear lever

19 Make the gearbox from two or three layers of ply glued together (fig 10). Chamfer the top edge using a file or sandpaper. The gear stick is ¼in (6mm) dowel with a wooden bead fitted on top. If you haven't got a wooden bead just paint the top of the dowel red.

20 Fit the other side of the bus in place and then fit ⅜×⅜in (9×9mm) wood all around the inside of the bus to hold the upper floor in place. Use the top of the staircase as a level.

21 Cut out the top deck (fig 11) and fit the seats. Your stairwell may need to be a different size if your staircase dimensions vary from mine.

22 Cut strips of ⅜in (9mm) ply, 1¼in (30mm) wide and glue and nail them in place beneath the floor between the wheel arches as bracing pieces. Fit the front one in front of the axle holes and the rear one behind the axle holes.

23 Make up the hood and radiator (fig 12). The radiator cap is made by drilling a ¼in (6mm) hole in a piece of ⅜in (9mm) ply, cutting a circle around it, and drilling a hole in the top of the radiator. A small piece of ¼in (6mm) dowel connects the two. I slit a piece of ⅛in (3mm) dowel lengthways for a decorative strip for the front, but anything will do.

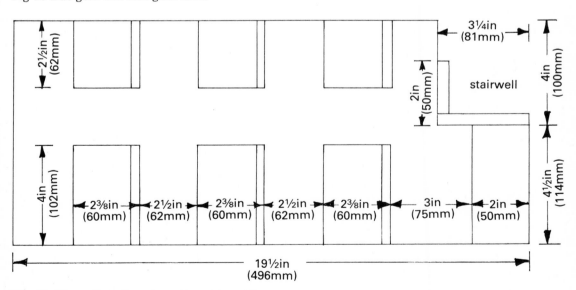

Fig 11 Plan of seating arrangement on the removable top deck

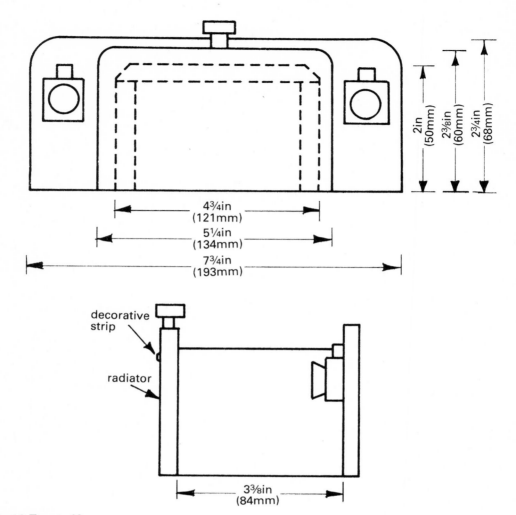

Fig 12 Front of bus

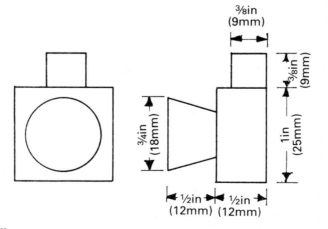

Fig 13 Bus headlamps

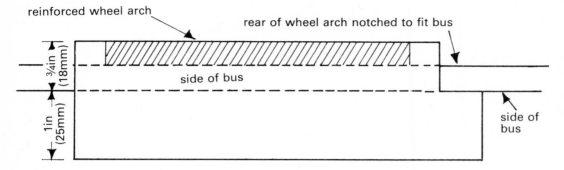

Fig 14 Front mudguard

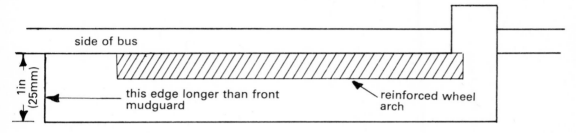

Fig 15 Rear mudguard

24 Make up the headlights (fig 13). I turned a piece of ¾in (18mm) dowel for the lens part using the method described in How To Do It (page 9), but you could leave it straight if you wanted to. Glue and fit them in place (see fig 12).

25 Make up the mudguards from ⅜in (9mm) ply (figs 14, 15 and fig 5), and fit them in place. The front of the front mudguard is ¾in (18mm) shorter than the corresponding piece on the rear mudguard.

26 Fit the ⅜in (9mm) ply School Bus sign and the ⅜in (9mm) ply roof over the driver's compartment.

27 Fit a ¾×½in (18×12mm) front bumper.

28 Paint the bus. I used gold paint for the 'General' lettering and the lights (see How To Do It, page 8). I painted my daughter's name on the side in lieu of an advertisement.

29 Finally fit the wheels. I used 4in (100mm) plastic spoked wheels with ¼in (6mm) steel axles and spring-loaded hub-caps; all are available in model shops.

SERVICE STATION

(shown in colour on page 88)

Most of the toys in this book are colour-fully painted but in the case of this service station I thought it would look better if it was just varnished. Make sure that you use a good quality ½in (12mm) plywood (tell your supplier that you are going to varnish it), and also try to get a small tube or tin of woodfiller which is a similar shade to the wood you are using.

1 Cut out the base, first floor and rooftop from ½in (12mm) ply (figs 1 and 2).
2 Cut out the three pieces for the sides and back of the 12in (305mm) long, 4in (100mm) wide, 5in (127mm) high ramps (figs 3 and 4) and glue and nail them together.
3 Cut out the 4in (100mm) wide slopes for the ramps making them a little longer

than required. Place them in position on the ramps and mark the angle of the mitre (fig 3). To do this, simply use a ruler and continue the base line of the ramps across the ramp slopes. Cut this mitre and then mark the top mitre in the same way but drawing your line vertically. The top edge of these ramps meets the floor above and should be a tight fit.
4 Cut eight 5in (127mm) lengths of 1×1in (25×25mm) ramin for the pillars; this is the normal type of hardwood sold in DIY shops.
5 You now have all the major pieces so it is a good idea to assemble them loosely so you can see how it looks. Start with the baseboard; put one ramp at the extreme rear left corner with the slope facing forwards. Place another ramp on the right

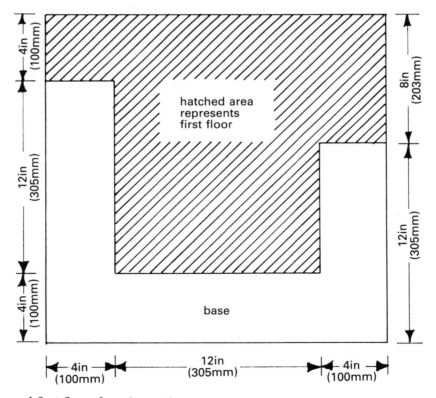

Fig 1 Base and first floor of service station

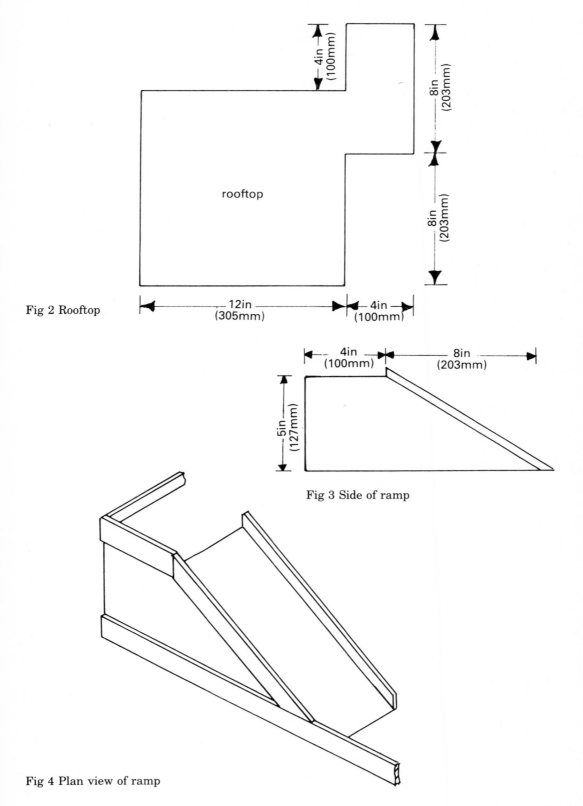

Fig 2 Rooftop

4in
(100mm)

8in
(203mm)

8in
(203mm)

rooftop

12in
(305mm)

4in
(100mm)

4in
(100mm)

8in
(203mm)

5in
(127mm)

Fig 3 Side of ramp

Fig 4 Plan view of ramp

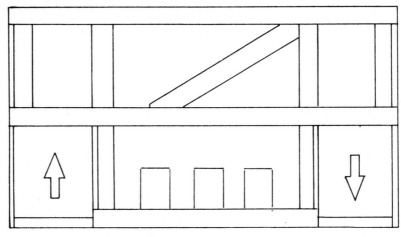

Fig 5 Front of service station

ramp down

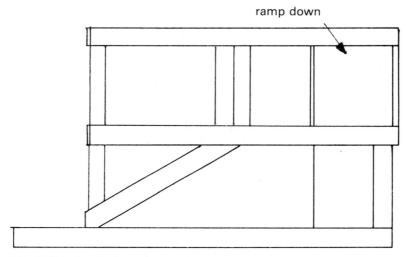

Fig 6 Side detail of service station

hand edge but 4in (100mm) from the rear (fig 5). Place the first floor on top of these two ramps. You will find that you will need two of the pillars under the front corners and one under the rear right hand corner to balance the floor. Place the remaining ramp in the right hand rear corner of the first floor with the slope pointing to the left (fig 6). The roof top sits on this and like the first floor, needs to be supported by the pillars (fig 7). Place two pillars under the front corners and one either side of the right hand ramp. The final pillar is under the rear left hand

corner. Now you can see the shape of the service station and before it is properly assembled, all that remains is to enhance its appearance.

6 Cut a 6in (152mm) wide, ¾in (18mm) deep notch out of the two front corners of the baseboard and two from the centre of the rear edge for the entrances and exits. Cut the small ramp (hatched area in fig 8) from ½in (12mm) ply making sure that the grain is running in the same direction as the baseboard. Glue these two small ramps to the baseboard.

7 Give the whole service station a thin

84

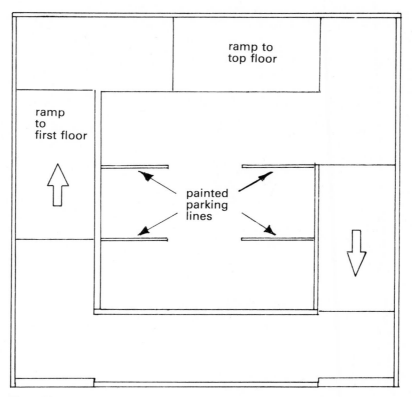

Fig 7 Plan view of top deck

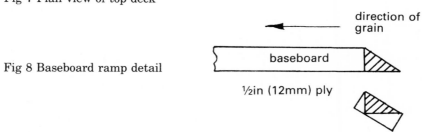

Fig 8 Baseboard ramp detail

direction of grain

baseboard

½in (12mm) ply

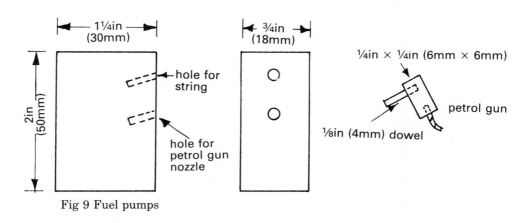

1¼in (30mm)

¾in (18mm)

2in (50mm)

hole for string

hole for petrol gun nozzle

¼in × ¼in (6mm × 6mm)

petrol gun

⅛in (4mm) dowel

Fig 9 Fuel pumps

coat of varnish to seal the wood prior to painting on the arrows, parking lines, 'IN' and 'OUT' signs and anything else you wish to include. If you make a mistake you can wipe the paint off varnished wood. Paint these signs on now.

8 Make the 2in (50mm) high fuel pumps from 1¼×¾in (30×18mm) hardwood (fig 9). Drill two ⅛in (4mm) holes for the fuel gun and the hose. Make the gun from ¼×¼in (6×6mm) ramin and ⅛in (4mm) dowelling. Put a spot of glue in the hose holes and poke a length of string in the holes using a pin. Glue and nail the pumps in position by nailing through the baseboard into the pumps.

9 Glue and nail the two ramps to the baseboard. Glue and nail 1×¼in (25×6mm) ramin to the inside edges of the ramps (it will be more difficult when the first floor is fixed). These pieces of ramin hide the end grain of the ply and form a small wall which prevents the cars

from sliding off.

10 Fit the first floor in position on top of the ramps and pillars.

11 Fit the remaining ramp and the roof top.

12 Cover all the exposed edges of the ply with the ¼×¼in (6×6mm) ramin (as for example in fig 4).

13 Using dry lettering print on the 'CAR PARK', and 'SERVICE STATION' signs.

14 Make a couple of barriers from 2×1¼×¾in (50×30×18mm) wood (fig 10). Cut a hole with the fretsaw for the ¼in (6mm) dowel pole to pass through. Make the 6in (152mm) pole from ¼in (6mm) dowel with a ¾in (18mm) piece of dowel as a counterweight. Drill a small hole through the ¼in (6mm) dowel and tap a panel pin through the side of the barrier stand and through the hole in the pole.

15 Give the whole of the service station several thin coats of varnish.

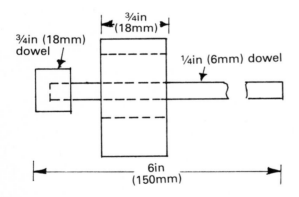
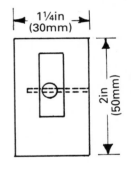

Fig 10 Barrier detail

Thatched Devon Cottage (page 92); Old-fashioned Bus (page 75)

DOLL'S KITCHEN

(shown in colour on page 70)

This kitchen is designed to a size suitable for the normal 11in (280mm) dolls.

1 Probably the best place to start is the rear wall. This is 20×13×⅛in (508×330×4mm) ply (fig 1). Mark out the position of the units and window on it and cut out the window (see How To Do It, page 7). It might be a good idea to lightly nail a 5¾×5in (146×127mm) piece of ⅛in (4mm) ply over the window position and then cut through this at the same time as the window. This will give you a window frame with panes exactly the same size as the openings in the rear wall.
2 Make up the carcase of the units (fig 2 and 3). Note the notch at the bottom of the base units and the 20×½in (508×12mm)

plinth. Before fitting the top of the base unit remember that a sink has to be fitted and so a hole has to be cut through this and through the worktop. Cut them out together. I used a small plastic lid from a pot of paint for the sink but almost any lid about ½in (12mm) deep will do.
3 The ceramic hot plate unit is 4×2½×⅛in (109×63×4mm) ply with the rings painted on, and the control panel made using either silver paint or kitchen foil.
4 Make up the doors of the unit (fig 4) using ¼in (6mm) ply for the back piece and ⅛in (4mm) ply for the raised outer edge and the inner insert. I did not use handles on the doors, but made them overlap at the bottom to give a fingerhold (fig 3).

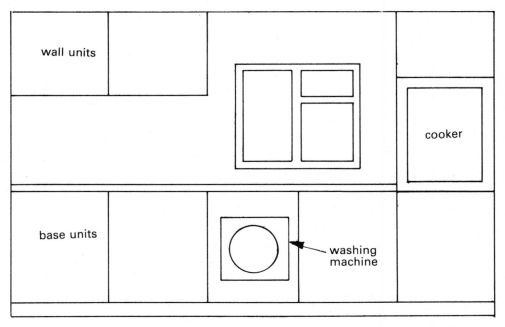

Fig 1 Back wall of kitchen showing position of the units

Grocer's Shop (page 104); Riding School with Horses, Riders, Land Rover and Horse Trailer (page 60); Service Station (page 82)

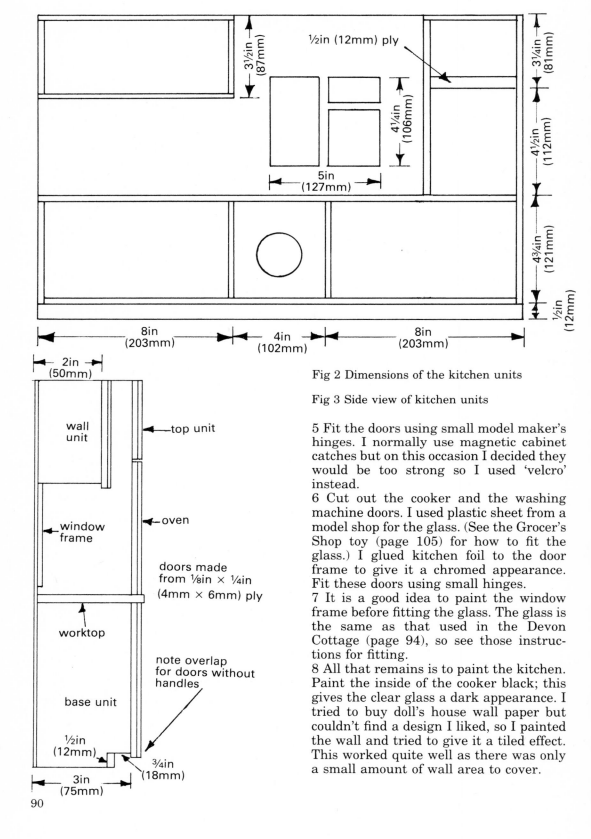

½in (12mm) ply

3½in (87mm)

4¼in (106mm)

5in (127mm)

3¼in (81mm)

4½in (112mm)

4¾in (121mm)

½in (12mm)

8in (203mm) 4in (102mm) 8in (203mm)

Fig 2 Dimensions of the kitchen units

Fig 3 Side view of kitchen units

2in (50mm)

wall unit

top unit

window frame

oven

doors made from ⅛in × ¼in (4mm × 6mm) ply

worktop

note overlap for doors without handles

base unit

½in (12mm)

¾in (18mm)

3in (75mm)

5 Fit the doors using small model maker's hinges. I normally use magnetic cabinet catches but on this occasion I decided they would be too strong so I used 'velcro' instead.

6 Cut out the cooker and the washing machine doors. I used plastic sheet from a model shop for the glass. (See the Grocer's Shop toy (page 105) for how to fit the glass.) I glued kitchen foil to the door frame to give it a chromed appearance. Fit these doors using small hinges.

7 It is a good idea to paint the window frame before fitting the glass. The glass is the same as that used in the Devon Cottage (page 94), so see those instructions for fitting.

8 All that remains is to paint the kitchen. Paint the inside of the cooker black; this gives the clear glass a dark appearance. I tried to buy doll's house wall paper but couldn't find a design I liked, so I painted the wall and tried to give it a tiled effect. This worked quite well as there was only a small amount of wall area to cover.

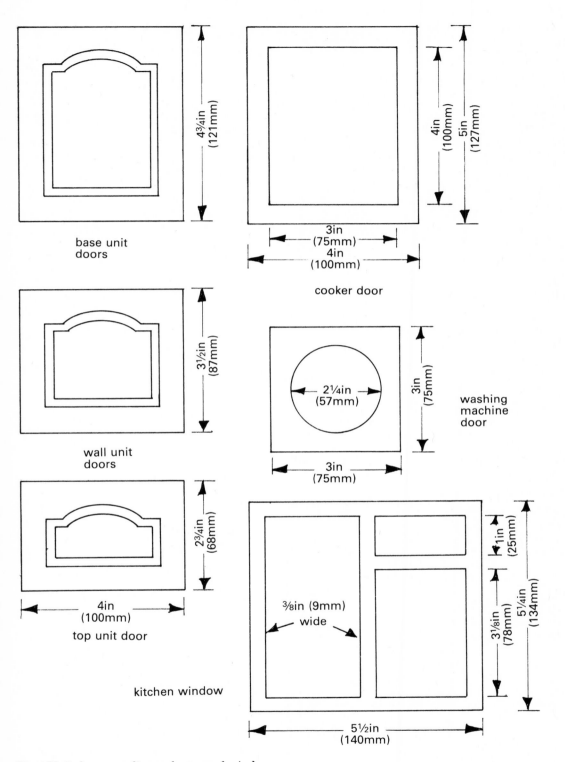

base unit
doors

cooker door

wall unit
doors

washing
machine
door

top unit door

kitchen window

Fig 4 Unit doors, appliance doors, and window
frame

THATCHED DEVON COTTAGE

(shown in colour on page 87)

I had bought the insulation board for the thatched roof from a timber merchant about two years before I started to make this toy. The problem was I didn't know how I was going to make the roof from the insulation board and the roof needed to be the final part of the toy. When I eventually took the plunge the roof was simple – the 'thatching' only requiring glueing to a framework.

1 Cut out the 22×13¼×¼in ((558×336× 6mm) ply for the back and front (figs 1 and 2).

2 Cut out the two 13¾×7×⅜in (348× 175×9mm) ply top side pieces, and two 14½×6¼×⅜in (362×158×9mm) bottom side pieces (fig 3).

3 Cut out two pieces of 21¼×14×¼in (540×356×6mm) ply for the ground floor and bedroom floor.

4 Cut out the stairwell in the upper floor (fig 4) and glue a length of ½×½in (12×12mm) wood on to the underside of the floor ¼in (6mm) from the edge. This will act as a guide for the sliding panel.

5 Cut out the window spaces on all the pieces (see How To Do It, page 7). Cut a ⅜in (9mm) notch on each edge of the back for the sliding panels. Glue a strip of 1×¼in (25×6mm) ply on the inside top edge of each of these panels (fig 5).

Fig 1 Front view of Devon cottage

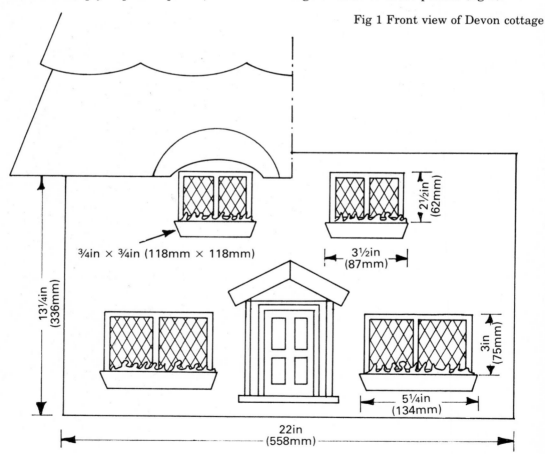

¾in × ¾in (118mm × 118mm)

3½in (87mm)

2½in (62mm)

13¼in (336mm)

3in (75mm)

5¼in (134mm)

22in (558mm)

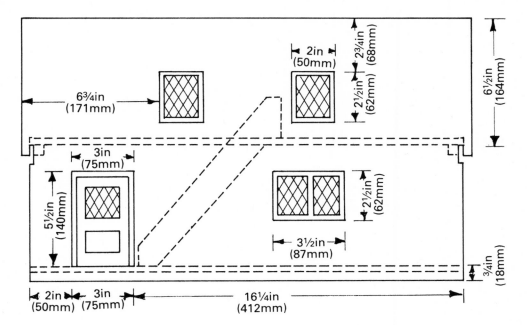

Fig 2 Rear of cottage

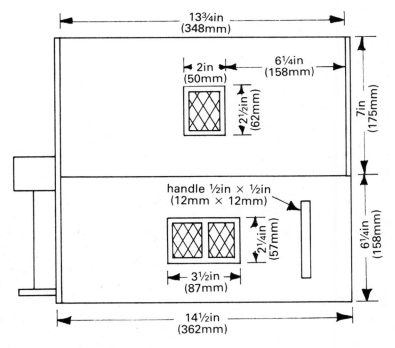

Fig 3 Side of cottage

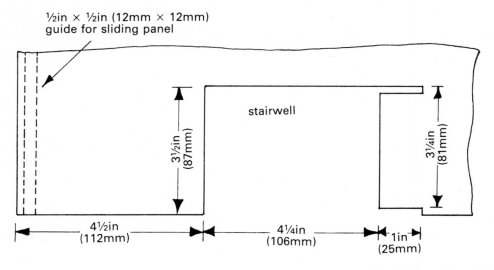

½in × ½in (12mm × 12mm) guide for sliding panel

stairwell

3½in (87mm)

3¼in (81mm)

4½in (112mm)

4¼in (106mm)

1in (25mm)

Fig 4 Upper floor stairwell

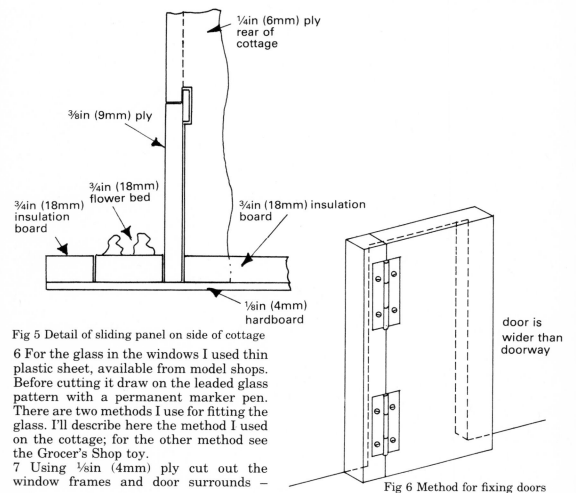

¼in (6mm) ply rear of cottage

⅜in (9mm) ply

¾in (18mm) flower bed

¾in (18mm) insulation board

¾in (18mm) insulation board

⅛in (4mm) hardboard

Fig 5 Detail of sliding panel on side of cottage

door is wider than doorway

Fig 6 Method for fixing doors

6 For the glass in the windows I used thin plastic sheet, available from model shops. Before cutting it draw on the leaded glass pattern with a permanent marker pen. There are two methods I use for fitting the glass. I'll describe here the method I used on the cottage; for the other method see the Grocer's Shop toy.

7 Using ⅛in (4mm) ply cut out the window frames and door surrounds –

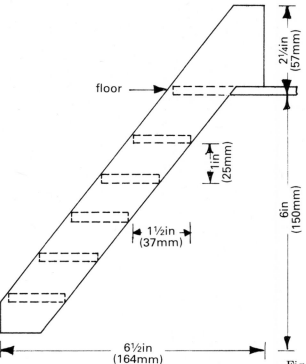

floor

2¼in (57mm)

1in (25mm)

1½in (37mm)

6in (150mm)

6½in (164mm)

Fig 7 Cottage staircase

these will fit over the openings you have already cut sandwiching the glass in between. Cut the glass with a craft knife or scissors and glue it over the window opening. Glue the window frame on top of the glass.

8 Cut both the doors from ¼in (6mm) and ⅛in (4mm) ply making them slightly larger than the door openings. Cut the door panels from the ¼in (6mm) ply and glue them on to the ⅛in (4mm) ply. This makes the total door ⅜in (9-10mm) thick. Fit the glass in the back door in the same manner as the windows.

9 Using small hinges fit the doors by screwing into the back of the door and, for the other half of the hinge, through a piece of ⅜in (9mm) ply and into the inside of the front of the house (see fig 6). This means that the doors will only open inwards.

10 Glue and nail the back and front to the two top sides and fit the floors in place.

11 Make the staircase (fig 7) from ¼in (6mm) ply and glue it in place. Note that it slides into the notches you have cut in the stairwell (fig 4).

12 Place the house on a 33×27×⅛in (840×686×4mm) hardboard base (fig 8). You now need to build this up with insulation board so that the sliding panels work (see fig 5). Cut the two flower beds from ¾in (18mm) ply (assuming your insulation board is ¾in (18mm), if it isn't adjust the thickness of ply accordingly). These beds help to keep the house in place and together with the ground floor, form a track for the sliding panels. The house is not fixed to the board permanently so don't worry that it is going to be too big. Glue a piece of ply to the hardboard for a path – I painted mine in a crazy paving pattern. The remainder is made from insulation board. Ordinary wood glue is all that is required to fix the board in place. I used ply for the flower beds because I thought the softer insulation board may wear out if it was continually being rubbed by the sliding panels. The flowers are irregular shapes of ⅜in (9mm) ply (fig 9). The trees (fig 10) are a couple of turned spires (see How To Do It, page 9).

13 Cut the window boxes from ¾×¾in

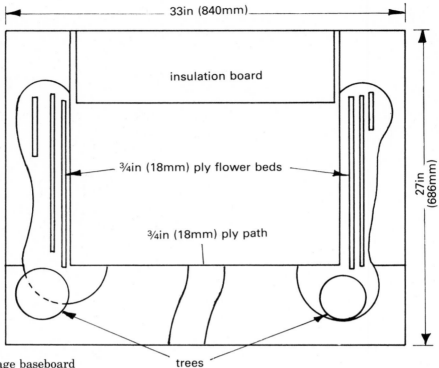

Fig 8 Cottage baseboard   trees

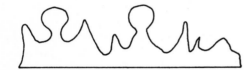

Fig 9 Flower beds

(18×18mm) wood and glue them to the front of the house (see fig 1). Make flowers as before and glue them to the window boxes. Paint them before fixing since it will be difficult to paint the backs of the flowers and these will be visible through the window.

14 Glue a piece of ½×½in (13×13mm) wood to each sliding panel as a pull handle (see fig 3).

15 To make the porch (fig 11) cut out a 4½×1¾×¼in (112×44×6mm) step, two trellises 5¼×1×¼in (134×25×6mm), the front triangular piece which is 4¼in (106mm) wide and 1¼in (32mm) high and a piece 3¾×1×¼in (93×25×6mm) for the porch ceiling. Cut out the diamond and triangular holes on the trellis with

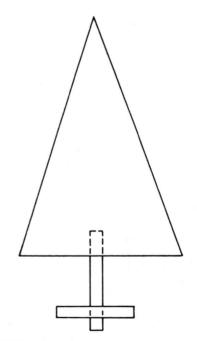

Fig 10 Trees

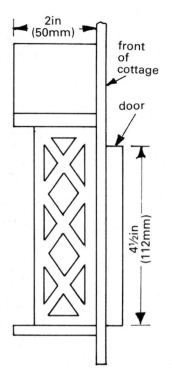

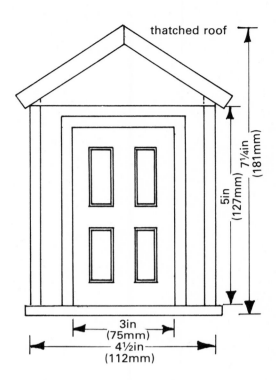

Fig 11 Side and front view of porch

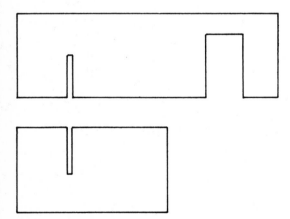

Fig 12 Internal wall design

the fretsaw (jigsaw). Glue and nail the trellis, step and ceiling together and then glue and nail the triangular piece in place. I cut out irregular shaped pieces of ¼in (6mm) ply and glued them to the trellis to simulate roses. Glue the porch to the front of the house and then cut the 'thatched' porch roof and glue it in place.
16 I have noticed that whatever shape or size the rooms of a doll's house are, the children can never get all the furniture they want into a particular room so on this house I decided to make the rooms flexible – more Japanese than Devon I suppose. I made a few internal walls (fig 12) of different sizes and left the children to make their own arrangements.

Now we come to the part I had been dreading – the roof. As it turned out, because the insulation board glued like wood, there were no problems.
17 The main part of the framework (fig 13) is made from 2×½in (50×13mm) wood, either ply or softwood will do, and is 23in (583mm) long by 14½in (362mm)

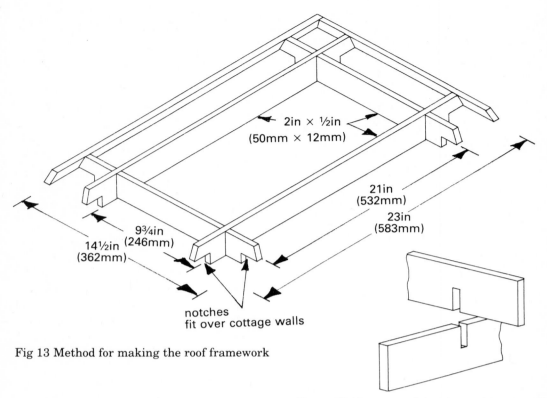

Fig 13 Method for making the roof framework

Fig 14 Half joint used for the roof framework

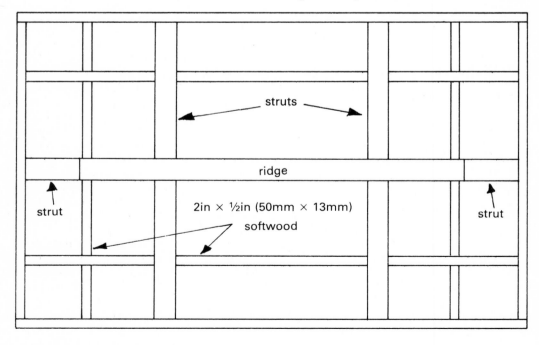

Fig 15 Plan of roof framework

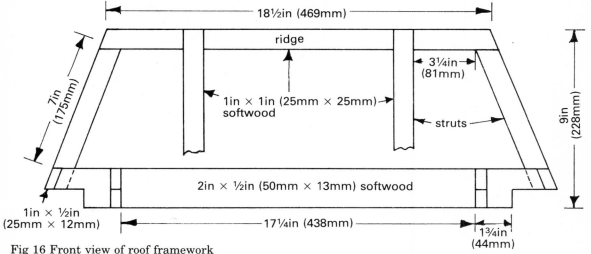

Fig 16 Front view of roof framework

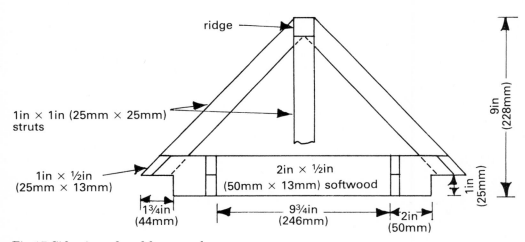

Fig 17 Side view of roof framework

wide and notched to fit over the walls of the house and hold the roof in place. I used simple half joints (fig 14) to fix the four pieces together.

18 Cut the 18½×1×1in (469×25×25mm) ridge and the two 8×1×1in (204×25× 25mm) side struts (figs 15, 16 and 17). These will help you to gauge the angle that the main pieces need to be cut at. Alternatively you can approximate the angle from the drawing. Don't worry about this, it only means that your roof may be slightly steeper or less steep than mine. Cut the ends of the frame to the angle of the roof and fix strips of ½in

(12mm) ply to the main 2×½in (50× 13mm) frame (fig 13 shows two pieces fixed). Cut all the struts notching them at one end to fit over the ½in (12mm) ply and at the other to fit over the ridge. Glue and nail them in place.

19 Cut the two ends of the roof from the insulation board (this is the full triangle in fig 18). I have not included sizes as they are better taken directly from your framework. Allow the roof to extend about 2in (50mm) lower than the top of the wall (see fig 1).

20 Cut out and fit the back of the roof. Cut out the front of the roof at the same time

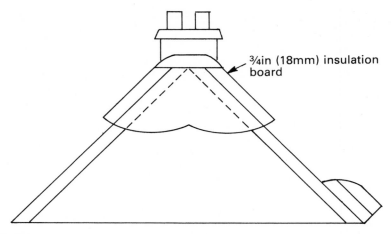

Fig 18 Side of thatched roof

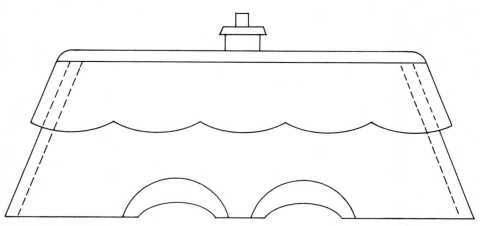

Fig 19 Front of thatched roof with window shaping

cutting the two crescent shapes above the windows (fig 19). The thatched dormer roofs are two thicknesses of insulation board glued to the main roof and rounded with sandpaper. I used a sander disc attachment on an electric drill although the insulation board sands easily by hand. Cut and glue the two top pieces of the gable ends in place. Cut and glue the top pieces on the front and back of the roof. At this point the top of the roof should be flat. If it isn't then cut or sand the insulation board level with the ridge.

21 Make the 3½×3×2in (87×75×50mm) chimney and fit the capping piece and ½in (12mm) dowel chimney pots to it.
22 Cut the insulation board for the top of the ridge, cutting a hole in the centre for the chimney to pass through. Glue the insulation board and chimney to the ridge. Sand all the edges round.
23 Paint the cottage. The insulation board I bought was straw coloured but it is easy to paint as the grass around the house shows.

TODDLER'S MERRY-GO-ROUND

(shown in colour on page 70)

This merry-go-round was the first toy my youngest daughter Krista played with by herself. To start with she would tentatively tap it with her finger setting it spinning, but it wasn't long before she was really bashing it!

1 Cut out a circle of ¼in (6mm) ply, 8¾in (222mm) in diameter with the fretsaw (figs 1 and 2) (see How To Do It, page 7).
2 From this circle cut out a 5¾in (146mm) inner circle which will become the base.
3 Cut a 1¼in (31mm) length of 1¼in (31mm) dowelling and chamfer one end (fig 1) with a file or sandpaper and fit it to the base to make a stand for the central pole. Drill a ½in (12mm) diameter hole in the centre of this stand and glue in a length of ½in (12mm) dowelling.
4 Drill into the top of the ½in (12mm) dowel using a ½in (12mm) drill bit until it forms a cup shape.
5 Drilling the angled holes for the four poles connecting the seating to the top of the merry-go-round is easy if you make a simple jig to guide the drill bit. All this need consist of is a block of wood with a hole drilled through it at the correct angle (fig 3), you can drill as many holes as you need until you get it right. When you are satisfied with your jig use it to drill the four holes in the seat and four holes in the 2½in (63mm) diameter, 1¼in (32mm)

thick top of the merry-go-round. For this top you can either use a single block of wood or two ½in (12mm) and one ¼in (6mm) piece of ply laminated together. Chamfer the top. Drill a ½in (12mm) hole in the top of the merry-go-round and fit a piece of ½in (12mm) dowelling. Round the protruding end of the dowel using sandpaper. This helps the merry-go-round to spin easily.
6 Cut the ¾in (18mm) holes for the seats using the fretsaw.
7 Cut the ⅜in (9mm) dowel connecting the seat to the top longer than required and glue them in position. Trim off the excess dowelling after the glue has dried.
8 Round the top of a 1¼in (31mm) length of 1¼in (31mm) dowel using a file or sandpaper as I did, or you could turn it with a drill (see How To Do It, page 9). This fits on to the top of the merry-go-round.
9 For the passengers use the same shape of people as used in the oil rig – just paint them in different colours. The small plastic figures which are sold with a variety of toys will also fit this toy.
10 Paint the merry-go-round. I painted the poles in a candy stripe pattern. To do this simply paint the poles with the lightest colour first and then twist adhesive tape around them and paint on the darker colour. When the tape is removed you will have nice crisp lines.

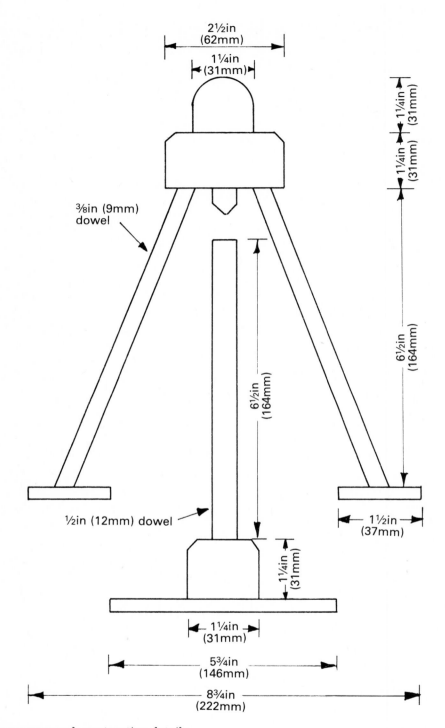

Fig 1 Merry-go-round construction details

Fig 2 Plan of merry-go-round

¾in (18mm) holes

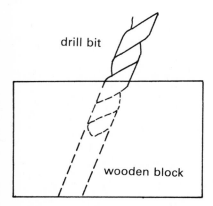

drill bit

wooden block

Fig 3 Simple drill jig

GROCER'S SHOP
(shown in colour on page 88)

This toy has a lot of educational value as it combines learning with play. I used cylindrical, rectangular and cuboid shapes of different colours for the stock. The idea is that children can group the 'packages' into different colours and count how many are in each group. They can then do the same for the different shapes and eventually decide how many 'packages' belong to two particular groups, say, red and cylindrical. This simple idea leads to quite difficult concepts that teenagers study in mathematics – not bad for a toy. These shapes for packaging are not out of place in a grocer's shop, although they would be in the more usual toy sweet shop and anyway, in a sweet shop the stock keeps disappearing! Another excellent reason for my choosing a grocer's rather than a sweet shop is that I am not very good at drawing the letter 'S' and there are two in sweet shop. Since the idea behind this book is to make toys easily I don't hesitate to miss out anything I think will be hard, no matter how trivial.

A more obvious educational benefit of the shop is the play value of buying, selling and giving change. This starts out as rather hit-and-miss, but it is surprising how soon a child begins to give the correct change – and complains when he isn't paid enough.

1 Cut out the 18×9½in (457×240mm) back and 10¾×9½in (273×241mm) sides from ⅜in (9mm) ply and *two* 18×9½in (457×240mm) fronts from ¼in (6mm) *and* ⅛in (4mm) ply (figs 1 and 2).
2 Temporarily fit the ⅜in (9mm) front on top of the ¼in (6mm) front with either adhesive tape or panel pins and cut out the windows and doorway (see How To Do It, page 7). This ensures they are exactly the same size. Keep the waste wood from the doorway as this will make the door.

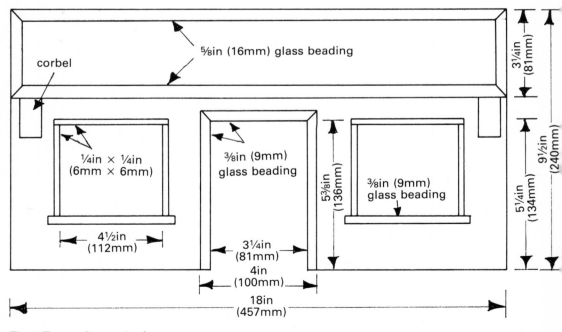

Fig 1 Front of grocer's shop

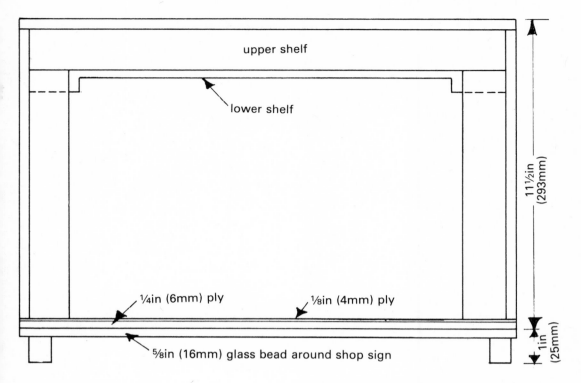

upper shelf

lower shelf

¼in (6mm) ply

⅛in (4mm) ply

11½in (293mm)

⅝in (16mm) glass bead around shop sign

1in (25mm)

Fig 2 Rear of shop

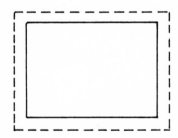

Fig 3 Shape of glass over the window frame

3 There are two methods I use for fitting the 'glass' in the windows. I'll describe here the method I recommend for the shop; for the other method see the Devon Cottage instructions. The windows of the shop are quite large so I use fairly strong plastic sheet bought from a model shop. The sheet I bought was approximately 12×9×½₀in (305×229×1mm). The ¼in (6mm) ply will be on the outside of the shop and the ⅛in (4mm) on the inside. On the inside of the ¼in (6mm) ply, draw a ¼in (6mm) border around the windows (fig 3). Plywood is made up of several layers; score along your border through the top layer using a craft knife (see How To Do It, page 8). Still using the craft knife cut out the top layer of ply in your

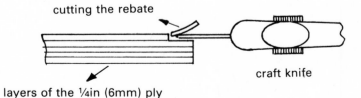

cutting the rebate

craft knife

layers of the ¼in (6mm) ply

Fig 4 Cutting the rebate in the plywood window frame

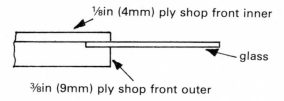

⅛in (4mm) ply shop front inner

glass

⅜in (9mm) ply shop front outer

Fig 5 Fitting the glass

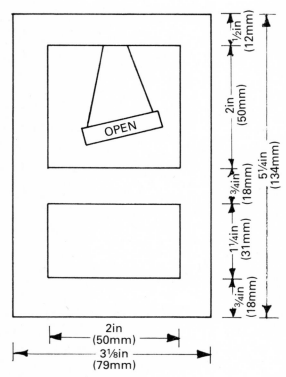

OPEN

½in (12mm)

2in (50mm)

5¼in (134mm)

¾in (18mm)

1¼in (31mm)

¾in (18mm)

2in (50mm)

3⅛in (79mm)

Fig 6 Shop door

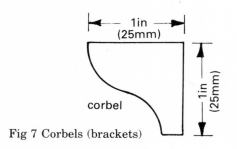

1in (25mm)

1in (25mm)

corbel

Fig 7 Corbels (brackets)

border (fig 4), on mine this was the exact thickness of the glass (fig 5). You may need to adjust yours depending on your ply and the plastic sheet. Cutting this rebate is not difficult and the whole process should not take more than a minute.

4 Whilst you are doing this make the door (fig 6). Like the shop front it is made from ⅛in (4mm) and ¼in (6mm) ply. Cut out the two panels on the ¼in (6mm) ply and the top one on the ⅛in (4mm) ply. Cut a similar rebate to the shop windows around the door window. The door will have to be trimmed a little to allow for the thickness of paint for it to open and close easily.

5 Place the glass over the rebate, mark where you need to cut on to the glass, then cut it with a craft knife.

6 At this stage I undercoated the window frames rather than leaving it until after the glass was fitted. You may like to paint the top coat as well but I was mixing my own colour and wanted to paint the whole shop in one go.

7 Paint the 'Grocer' sign on the glass before fitting it. I hadn't thought about painting on the glass until I had finished the toy and then I did a dummy run on a piece of spare glass and it was far easier than painting it in *situ*. I used gold paint (see How To Do It, page 8) and outlined it in black.

8 Glue ⅝in (16mm) glass beading to the front of the shop for the framework of the shop name. DIY shops sell this bead by the foot. Use ⅜in (9mm) glass bead for the architraving around the door and for the window sills. The window frames are ¼×¼in (6×6mm) wood; again this is sold by the foot. Cut out the two corbels (brackets) (fig 7) from 1×1in (25×25mm) wood and glue them in place.

9 Fit the door using small hinges screwed into the back of the door and the inside of the shop.

10 Glue and nail the back, sides and front together.

11 Fit the shelves. The top shelf is made from ½in (12mm) ply. The bottom one was also made from ply only it was cut in one piece using the fretsaw (jigsaw) (see How To Do It, page 7). (See fig 2.)

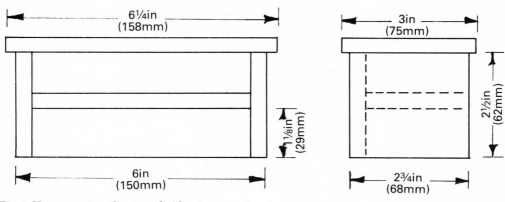

Fig 8 Shop counter, front and side view

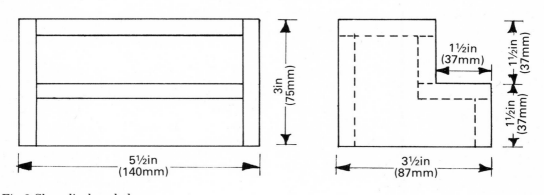

Fig 9 Shop display shelves

12 Cut out a 15×20in (381×508mm) baseboard from ³⁄₈in (9mm) ply.

13 Undercoat the shop and baseboard. Place the shop on the baseboard and mark its position. This is because the floor of the shop is a different colour from the outside pavement. I gave the shop floor a chequered pattern. If you want to do the same, see the Alice Chess Board on page 58 for instructions.

14 Draw your shop name on a piece of paper and then place it in position on the shop; draw over it pressing very firmly. This leaves an imprint in the paint which acts as a guide for your sign painting. I used gold paint outlined in red and then edged on one side in black. You will need a good quality art brush for this (see How To Do It, page 8).

15 Fit the shop to the base by glueing and nailing.

16 Make up the simple shop counter (fig 8) and two shop display shelves (fig 9).

17 Make packages from pieces of dowelling, square or rectangular wood and paint them in primary colours.

18 As a finishing touch make an 'OPEN/ CLOSED' sign. I used the letters that are supplied with blank video tapes – I've never found another use for them – alternatively use dry lettering. Hang the sign with a drawing pin. The first thing my daughter Ulenka did was to open the shop.

CASTLE
(shown in colour on page 69)

This castle is the first toy I ever made and at the time of writing is about eight years old. I had received one of the 'playpeople' toys (see photograph) as a promotional offer and I designed the castle to scale around that one figure. At the time I didn't have a fretsaw (jigsaw) so almost the entire castle was made using a coping saw. I started the toy by making the guardhouse to see if I could cut out the crenelles and windows; if this is your first toy you may want to do the same. I wanted to make a large castle but it had to pass through normal doorways so the overall size was kept to 24in (610mm). A problem that I foresaw that may also affect you was storage. I needed to be able to put the castle in the loft from time to time but because loft openings are quite small, I made the castle so that it would dismantle, using ¼in (6mm) dowelling to hold the sides together rather than glue and panel pins.

1 Cut out the front (fig 1), internal wall (fig 2), two sides (fig 3) and the back (fig 4). Before cutting out the crenelles, windows and doors, temporarily assemble using adhesive tape to check that they fit together correctly. When you are satisfied cut out the crenelles etc.

2 Glue and nail the ½×½in (13×13mm) courtyard supports to the back, front and sides.

3 Glue and nail the ½in (12mm) ply ramparts to the front and two sides.

4 If you want to be able to dismantle the castle, fit the 1×1in (25×25mm) wood to the front and two sides.

5 Cut the back into three pieces (fig 4).

6 Assemble the castle again and drill ¼in (6mm) holes through the bottom and top pieces of the back of the castle into the 1×1in (25×25mm) wood you have already fixed to the castle sides. The centre piece of the back is not drilled. It is removable so that the child can gain access to the banquet hall and kitchen/

armoury. I made mine a tight fit but the child can use the windows as finger holds to pull this piece off, but if you prefer use magnetic cabinet catches to hold it in place. Drill similar holes through the sides into the 1×1in (25×25mm) wood fitted to the front, and through the internal wall into the 1×1in (25×25mm) wood fitted to the side. Dismantle the castle and glue ¼in (6mm) dowelling into the holes in the 1×1in (25×25mm) wood leaving about ½in (12mm) protruding. When the glue has dried reassemble the castle and trim off the excess dowelling. You will now be able to assemble and dismantle the castle whenever you like.

7 Cut out the 6¼×5×½in (158×127×12mm) ply drawbridge. Drill a ¼in (6mm) hole in each edge of the drawbridge as illustrated in fig 5. You now need to drill a ⁵⁄₁₆in (8mm) hole in each buttress so that the drawbridge opens at floor level. If you are unsure of measuring this accurately, I would suggest cutting the buttresses 12in (305mm) long which will allow 1in (25mm) below the bottom of the castle and 1in (25mm) above the finishing height of the buttress. You can then fit the ¼in (6mm) dowel into the holes of the drawbridge and buttresses and move the buttresses up or down by up to 1in (25mm) until it opens perfectly; mark the position and cut the buttresses to size. Fix the buttresses with the drawbridge in place by nailing through the castle wall into the buttresses.

8 Cut out the pieces for the ramp (fig 6) and glue and nail them together.

9 Cut out the 23½×21¾×¼in (598×552×6mm) ply courtyard.

10 Cut out the two 8×8×¼in (203×203×6mm) ply rear battlements (fig 7).

11 Cut out the 8×7×¼in (203×178×6mm) ply bedroom floor (fig 7).

12 Cut out the 23½×8×¼in (598×203×6mm) ply banquet hall floor.

13 Cut out the two 8×4½×¼in (203×112×6mm) ply bedroom walls and

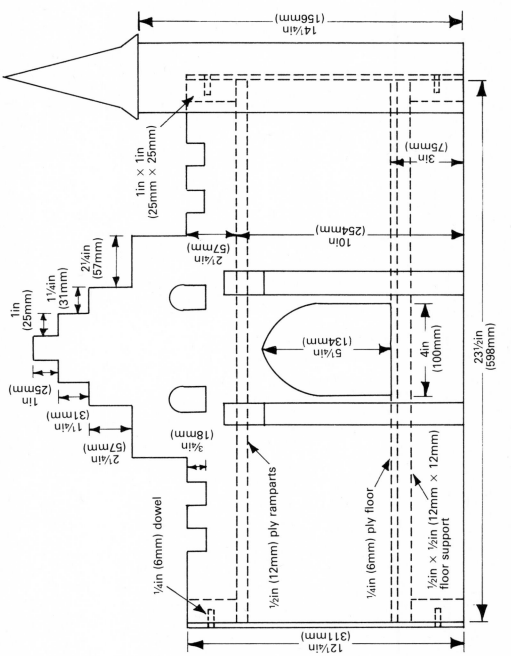

Fig 1 Front detail of the castle

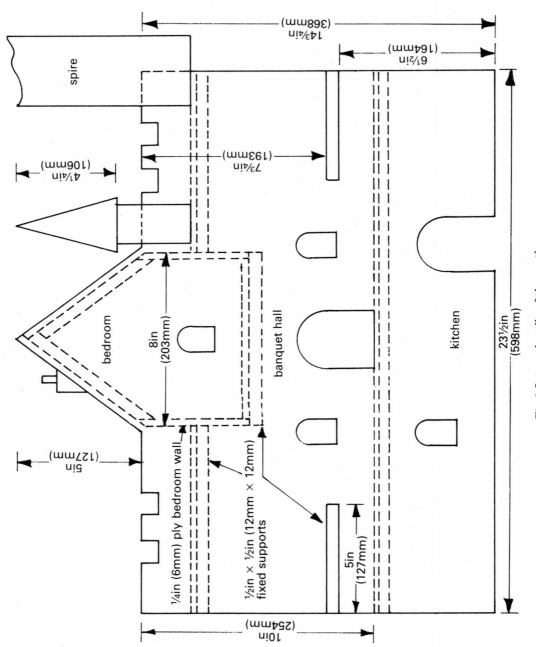

Fig 2 Internal walls of the castle

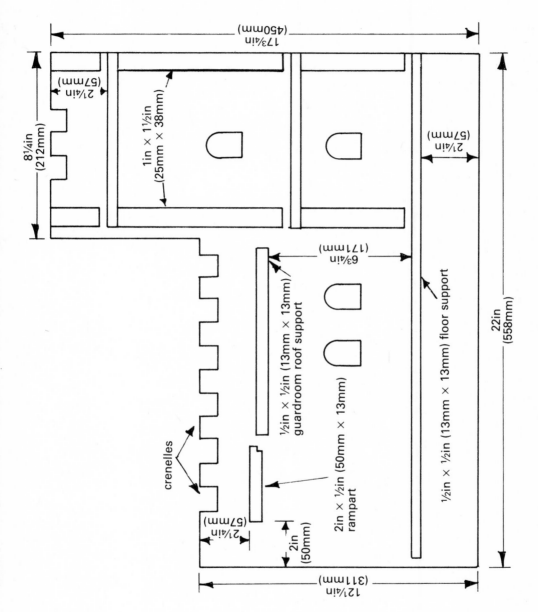

Fig 3 Side of the castle viewed from the inside

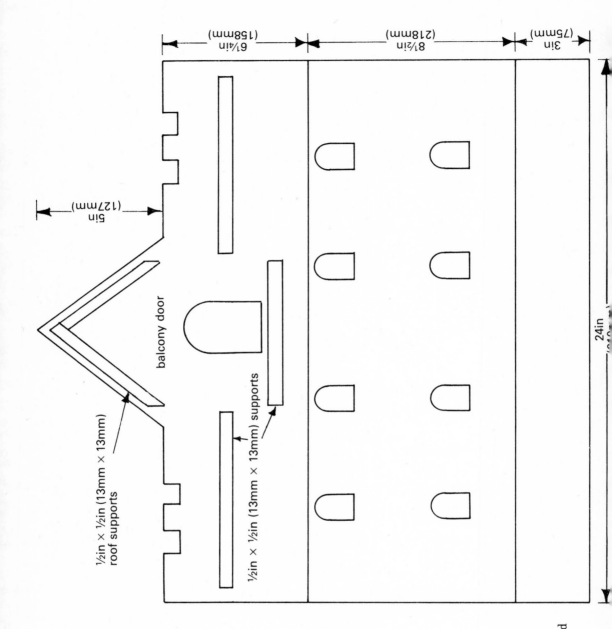

Fig 4 Rear of the castle viewed
from the inside

6¹⁄₂in (158mm)

8¹⁄₂in (218mm)

3in (75mm)

5in (127mm)

24in

½in × ½in (13mm × 13mm) roof supports

balcony door

½in × ½in (13mm × 13mm) supports

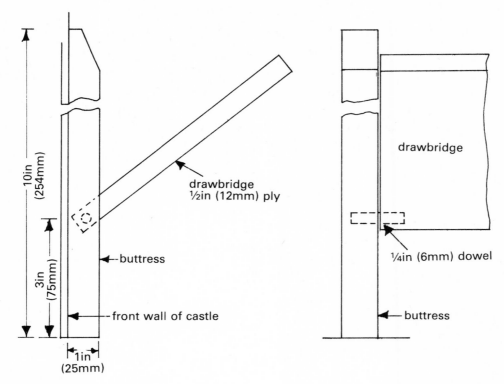

Fig 5 Drawbridge detail

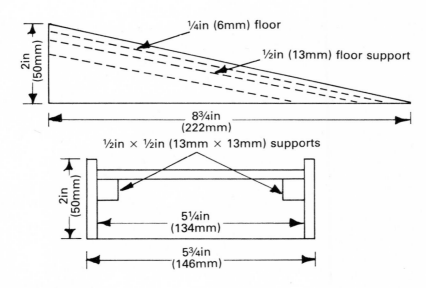

Fig 6 Ramp to drawbridge

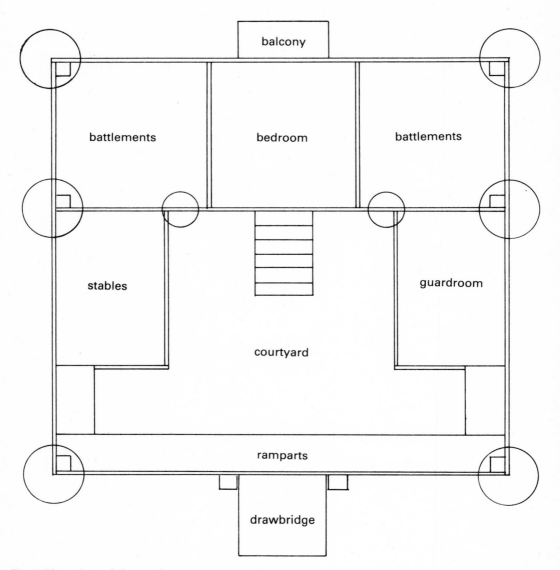

Fig 7 Plan view of the castle

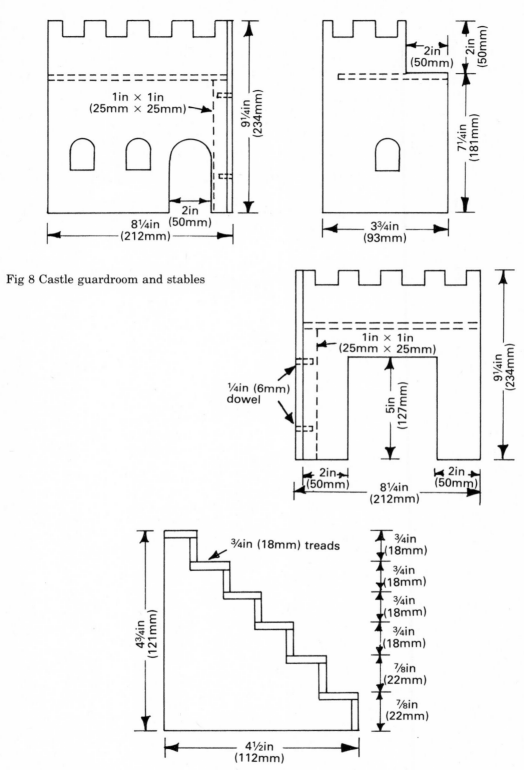

Fig 8 Castle guardroom and stables

Fig 9 Staircase

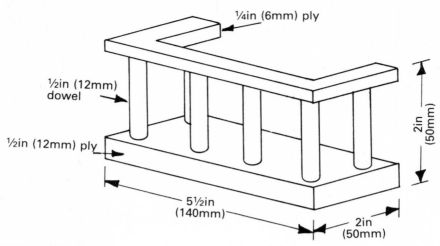

½in (12mm) dowel →

½in (12mm) ply →

¼in (6mm) ply

2in (50mm)

5½in (140mm)

2in (50mm)

Fig 10 Balcony details

chamfer the tops of these walls with a file or sandpaper to the same angle as the roof supports (fig 2). The combination of the roof supports, battlements, bedroom floor and bedroom floor supports keeps the walls firmly in place when assembled.

14 Cut out the two pieces of ¼in (6mm) ply for the roof. One will be 8×7in (203×178mm) and the other 8×6¾in (203×171mm). Fix a chimney made from a piece of 1×1in (25×25mm) wood with a piece of ¼in (6mm) dowel for the chimney pot, on to the larger side of the roof. The chimney acts as a handle for removing the roof. Fit a strip of ½×½in (13×13mm) wood near to the bottom inside edge of each roof side to prevent them from sliding down.

15 Cut out the guardroom and stable pieces (fig 8) and fit the ½×½in (13×13mm) roof supports and the 1×1in (25×25mm) wood. As before, drill through the side into the 1×1in (25×25mm) wood for the ¼in (6mm) dowelling. Cut two 8×5¾×¼in (203×146×6mm) ply roofs and glue a strip of ½×½in (13×13mm) wood to each of them for a handle.

16 Cut out the staircase sides (fig 9) and fit the 3×¾×¼in (75×18×6mm) ply treads and also fit the risers. Note that two of the risers are 3×⅞in (75×23mm) whilst the other four are 3×¾in (75×

18mm) to bring the top of the staircase to floor level.

17 To make the bedroom balcony cut 5½×2in (140×50mm) pieces of ½in (12mm) and ¼in (6mm) ply (fig 10). Hold them together with adhesive tape and mark the position for the railings. Drill through the ½in (12mm) ply into the ¼in (6mm) ply. Try not to drill all the way through the ¼in (6mm) ply – use a piece of tape wrapped around the drill bit as a depth gauge, Cut six 1⅞in (47mm) long lengths of ¼in (6mm) dowel and glue them into the balcony floor and the handrail. Glue and nail the balcony in place.

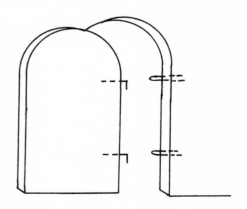

Fig 11 Method for hanging doors using dressmaker's pins

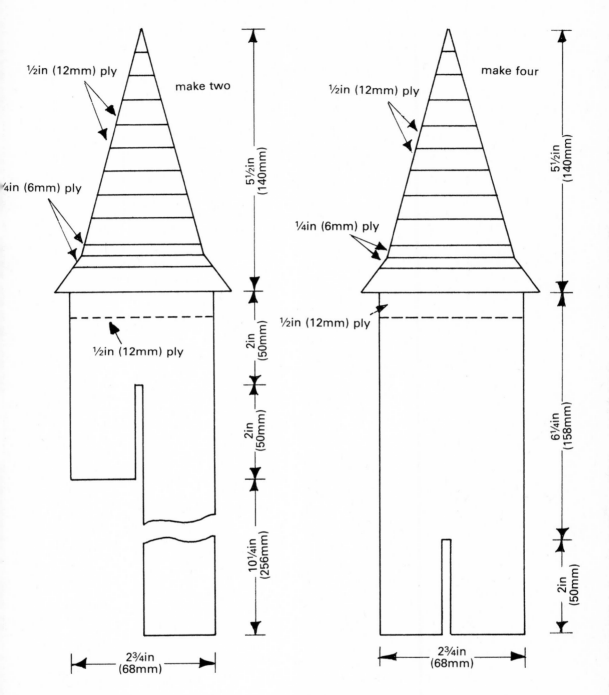

½in (12mm) ply

make two

¼in (6mm) ply

5½in (140mm)

½in (12mm) ply

2in (50mm)

2in (50mm)

10¼in (256mm)

2¾in (68mm)

½in (12mm) ply

make four

¼in (6mm) ply

5½in (140mm)

½in (12mm) ply

6¼in (158mm)

2in (50mm)

2¾in (68mm)

Fig 12 Front spires

Fig 13 Rear spires

117

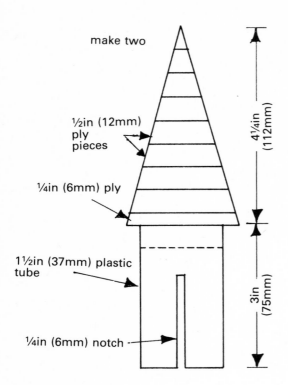

make two

½in (12mm)
ply
pieces

¼in (6mm) ply

1½in (37mm) plastic
tube

¼in (6mm) notch

4¼in (112mm)

3in (75mm)

Fig 14 Small spires

Fig 15 Simple method for making spires

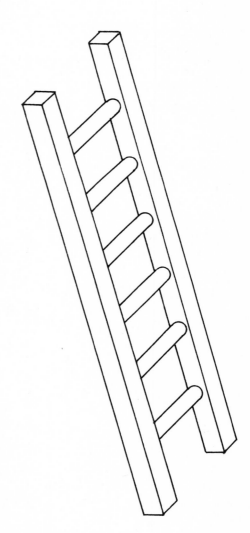

18 To hang the doors I used dressmaker's pins for the hinges. Cut the heads off two pins and bend them into a 'U' shape (fig 11), then using a pair of pliers push them into the door jamb. Cut the heads off two more pins and bend them into an 'L' shape. The 'L' shape slots into the 'U' shape and the doors are hung in seconds. For an alternative method see the Grocer's Shop, page 106.

19 The spires (figs 12, 13 and 14) are made by laminating discs of ½in (12mm) and ¼in (6mm) ply and then turning them (see How To Do It, page 9). The bottom piece of the spire is the same diameter as the inside of the turrets which are made from plastic rainwater pipe (available from any DIY store or builders merchant). The spire will then slot into the turret. The turrets are notched to fit over the walls of the castle. I used 1½in (37mm) tube for the two small spires and 2¾in (68mm) tube for

Fig 16 Castle ladder

the remaining six. The inside quadrants of the two front turrets are cut away below the top of the ramparts – they will not fit otherwise. The notches can be cut with a craft knife.

As an alternative you could use cardboard tubes and it is also possible to make simple spires from cardboard. Cut out a circle of cardboard then cut a slice from it (fig 15) and join the two cut edges with adhesive tape. A larger spire with the centre cut out can be joined to the first to give the 'witch's hat' shape illustrated. Make some extra spires if you use this method as they will not be very strong. A method I have used successfully is to fill these cardboard spires with epoxy resin and then set the turrets inside the spires. When the epoxy resin has set the cardboard is peeled away. However, I prefer the wooden spires.

20 Make a couple of ladders (fig 16) from $\frac{1}{2} \times \frac{1}{2}$in (13×13mm) wood, drilling $\frac{1}{4}$in (6mm) holes at $1\frac{1}{4}$in (31mm) intervals and then glueing $1\frac{1}{2}$in (38mm) lengths of $\frac{1}{4}$in (6mm) dowel into them for the rungs.
21 Paint the castle. For the textured finish I mixed sawdust with the undercoat paint, but I have since discovered that a better method is to use textured paint. If you want a gloss finish use the textured paint as an undercoat but if you prefer the more natural looking matt finish, add some black paint dye until you get the shade of grey you want and then the castle can be painted in one coat.
22 Attach two small lengths of chain to the drawbridge and the front castle wall making it the correct length for the drawbridge to lower to the ramp.

The castle is now ready for the army to move in.

MEDIEVAL CATAPULT

(shown in colour on page 69)

This is not really a toy that I wanted to make! When I was at the age for playing with castles and soldiers, the father of the boy next door made him a pair of wooden pistols and a pair of wooden rifles. They had copper barrels and fired 2in (50mm) lengths of ½in (12mm) dowelling. We though they were brilliant! They were accurate enough to knock a can off a bookshelf from across the room and we used them as cannons in our war games. I had wanted to make some of these guns to go with the castle but my wife was very much against it. So instead I made this medieval catapult or mangonel which is good at knocking over soldiers, but hopeless for knocking down tin cans!

1 For the frame, cut out two pieces of 8×¾×½in (203×18×12mm) ply and two pieces of 5×¾×½in (127×18×12mm) ply for the base.
2 Cut a 1in (25mm) wide × ¼in (6mm) deep notch in each of the longer pieces for the uprights (figs 1 and 2).
3 Cut out the 4×1×½in (100×25×12mm)

uprights and glue and nail them in place.
4 Drill a ⁵⁄₁₆in (8mm) hole in each of the two sides for the catapult.
5 Cut out the catapult from ½in (12mm) ply (fig 3). Drill the three ⅛in (3mm) holes for the ⅛in (3mm) dowelling pegs. The elastic band fits over these, and by having more than one, the range can be varied. Drill a hole in each side and fit a piece of ¼in (3mm) dowel.
6 Cut a piece of 2×1×½in (50×25×12mm) ply for the crosspiece between the uprights. With the catapult in place, fit this crosspiece. Note that it fits at an angle so that the catapult beam hits it flat.
7 Glue and nail the 8in (203mm) long pieces on top of the 5in (127mm) pieces.
8 Paint the whole catapult.
9 Fit a small hook in the back of the crosspiece to hold the elastic band. Hook the elastic band around this hook and the catapult pegs (fig 1).
10 Either cut discs from ½in (12mm) ply or use short lengths of 1in (25mm) diameter dowelling as missiles.

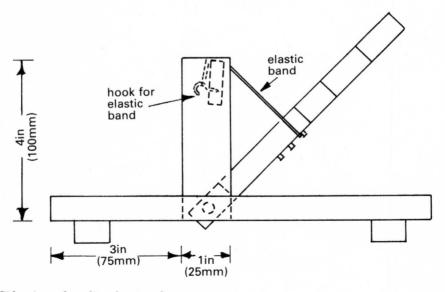

Fig 1 Side view of medieval catapult

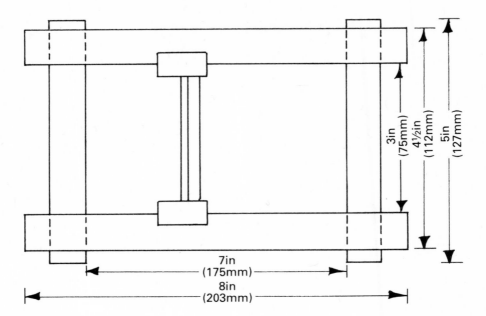

Fig 2 Plan of catapult frame

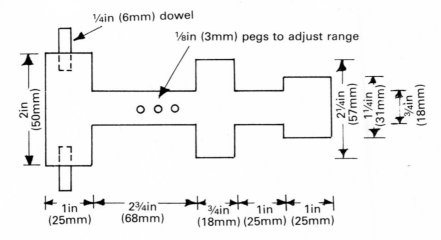

Fig 3 Catapult shape

COATHANGERS
(shown in colour on page 34)

For most children the best place for a coathanger is on the floor as this is about the only place that a coat will ever end up on it. You could try making these novelty coathangers to encourage your children to hang their clothes up . . . no guarantees!

1 Mark out the outline (fig 1 or 2) on ¼in (6mm) ply. Make sure the hook part will fit the rail in your wardrobe – the hook can easily be modified.

2 Cut out the outline with the fretsaw (jigsaw).

3 Paint the coathanger. In the case of the lifeguard I used kitchen foil for the helmet and breast plate, I also used gold paint for the badge on the helmet (see How To Do It, page 8).

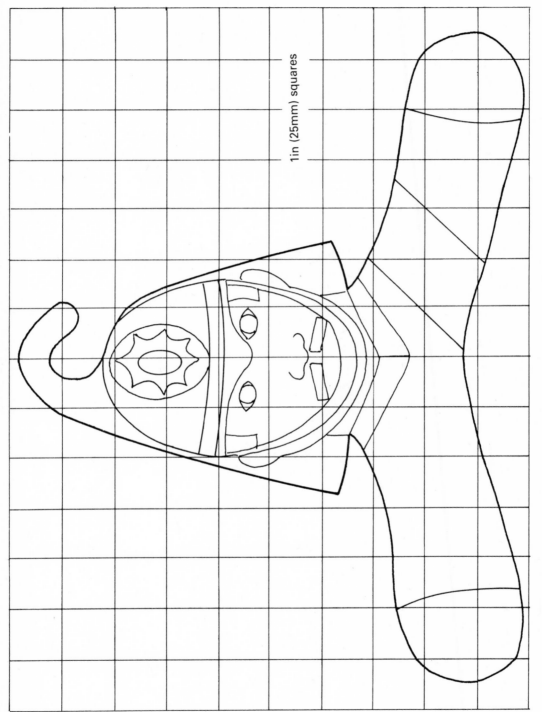

1in (25mm) squares

Fig 1 Lifeguard coathanger

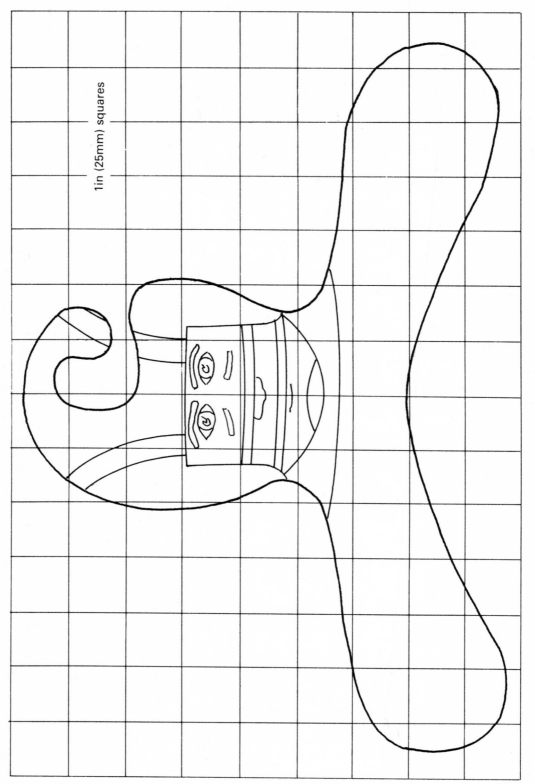

1in (25mm) squares

Fig 2 American footballer coathanger

ST GEORGE AND THE DRAGON

(shown in colour on page 69)

Throughout the ages dragons have had pretty hard press. They are supposed to be guilty of all sorts of despicable deeds, but if we read some of the stories the dragon does seem to be very badly done by. Take knights for example; there was nothing they liked better than rescuing a damsel in distress, which usually involved killing a dragon or two in the process, and then picking up a nice reward. George here was even made a saint. There was little Bilbo Baggins too. He robbed Tolkein's dragon Smaug of his treasure. However, probably the most hard done by dragon of all was Wagner's Fafner. He was one of the giants who built Valhalla and was paid by Wotan with a hoard of gold. Rather than put his gold in the bank, Fafner chose to use a magic helmet to change himself into a dragon to guard his fortune. Then in comes Siegfried and kills Fafner just for the fun of it.

Anyway, I thought it was about time dragons got their own back so I made this dragon 1in (25mm) thick whilst St George is only ½in (12mm) thick; this gives the dragon an advantage. St George and the dragon are rolled at each other and usually St George comes off worst!

The Dragon

1 Glue two pieces of ½in (12mm) ply together and transfer the outline of the dragon on to them (fig 2).
2 Cut out the dragon using either the fretsaw (jigsaw) or a coping saw (see How To Do it, page 7).
3 Drill ⁵⁄₁₆in (8mm) axle holes in the feet.
4 Cut out eight 2in (50mm) diameter wheels from ½in (12mm) ply (four of these are for St George). (See How To Do It, page 9.)
5 Undercoat and paint the dragon and the inside face of the wheels.
6 Fit the wheels on ¼in (6mm) dowel axles. Paint the outside face of the wheels.

St George

1 Transfer the outline of St George on to a single thickness of ½in (12mm) ply and cut it out (fig 3).
2 Drill the two ⁵⁄₁₆in (8mm) axle holes and a ¼in (6mm) hole for the arm. Do not drill all the way through. Use adhesive tape as a gauge.
3 Cut out the right arm and drill a ¼in (6mm) hole through the hand for the lance (fig 1).
4 Cut a 8in (203mm) length of dowel for the lance. Drill a ¼in (6mm) hole into (not through) a piece of ½in (12mm) ply and cut a ½×½in (12×12mm) square around it. Glue the end of the dowel lance into the cube of ply and cut the sides into a blunt point. Doing it this way you can hold the shaft while you cut the point. Drill a ¼in (6mm) hole in the arm and glue a small length of ¼in (6mm) dowel into it. Glue the lance into the hand.
5 Paint St George and the inside face of the wheels. Fit the wheels in place with ¼in (6mm) dowel axles and paint the outside face.
6 Fit the arm in place. If you want it to be movable, do not glue it. Let battle commence!

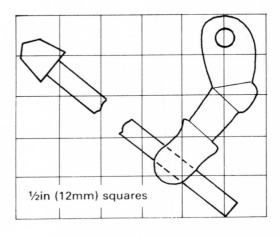

½in (12mm) squares

Fig 1 St George's right arm with lance

1in (25mm) squares

Fig 2 The Dragon

126

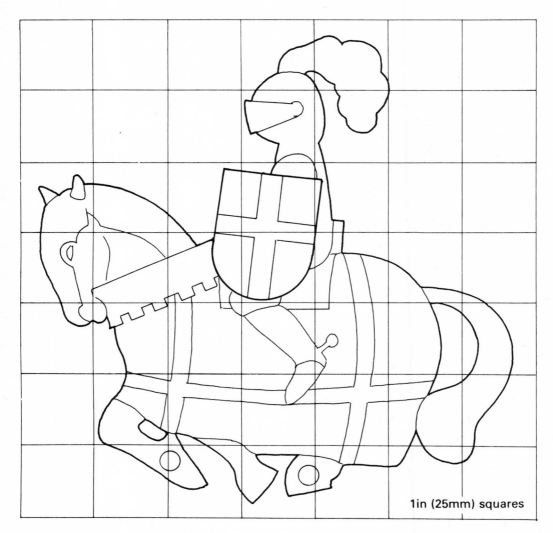

1in (25mm) squares

Fig 3 St George

TOYS FROM SCRAP WOOD

(shown in colour on pages 34 and 70)

If you have made any of the toys in this book you are more than likely to have some scrap wood left over. Rather than throw it away, why not make some small toys out of it, either for your own children or for friends, and some are especially useful for giving to school fêtes or summer fairs.

There are already some ideas for using up waste wood to be found in the book, for example the Stacking Beefeater. But why not try making some of the following toys such as the Fishing Game or the numerous Victorian toys, all of which are very colourful and effective yet extremely simple to make.

Making wooden letters and numbers is also a very good way of using up waste wood. You could trace around the letters of the alphabet using an ABC book as a guide, then transfer the designs to the wood and cut them out. Children can learn to match up the letters with those in the book. Why not cut out just the letters of your child's name and place them on their bedroom door or above their coat-hook. Alternatively, just let them play with the letters and they will soon learn how to spell their name.

It would also be very easy to make a simple adding game by cutting out numbers and a plus and minus sign together with an equals sign. You can then set your children simple sums and they will have to find the right number for the answer.

FISHING GAME

(shown in colour on page 34)

When I was between the ages of fifteen and sixteen I had a vacation job at the local fairground. Most of the time I worked on the rides but occasionally I worked for the stall holders and I soon realised that there was a trick to almost all the games. The fishing game was on a nearby stall and was operated by the owner. Each fish had a number painted on the underside, the idea being to get a score from three fish of say ten to win a prize, and exactly five to win *any* prize. About one in five people managed to score ten, but the prize was only the equivalent of those found in Christmas crackers. To score exactly five was very difficult as the only way to do it was with either a 1, 2 and 2 or a 1, 1 and 3. In order to restrict the number of prizes given out, there was only one fish with the number one on it!

Notwithstanding this trickery, this fishing game is excellent for school fêtes or for children to play with in the garden paddling pool.

1 Cut out the fish from ply (fig 1). I used ¾in (18mm) ply because that was the length of the screw thread on the cup hooks. Either of the fish shapes will do; the simpler one may be better if you are not yet proficient with the fretsaw or coping saw, or if you are going to make a lot. Make sure that they are almost identical, including the painting, and that the cup hooks face in the same direction (a dead giveaway!).

2 Use a 'magic marker' or paint to put the numbers on the underside. The cup hooks are available from ironmonger's or DIY shops.

3 The fishing rods can be made from pieces of dowel or bamboo canes. For the hooks use circular brass curtain hooks, again available at ironmonger's or DIY shops.

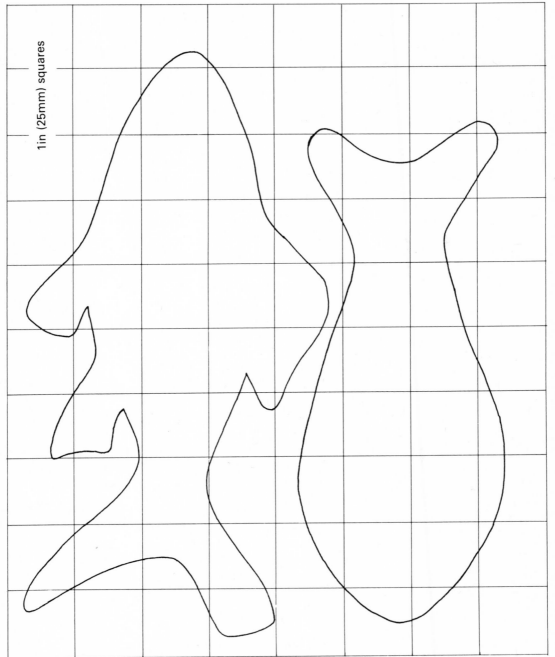

1in (25mm) squares

Fig 1 Fish shapes

VICTORIAN TOYS

(all shown in colour on pages 34 and 70)

Chromatrope (fig 1)
The Victorians were fond of giving simple toys long names. This is just a simple spinner but it does have a rather special quality. If you paint the chromatrope in the suggested colours, which are the colours of the spectrum, when you spin it, the colours cancel each other out and it turns white. This is an excellent toy to make for school fêtes as it is almost as easy to make a dozen as it is to make one. Use ⅛in (4mm) or ¼in (6mm) ply.

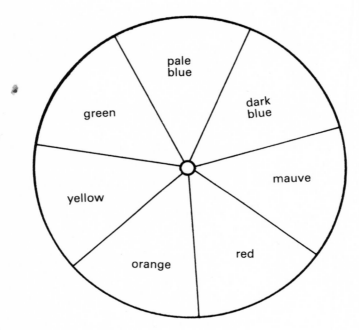

Fig 1 Chromatrope

Thaumatrope (fig 2)
This is another optical illusion. The idea is to paint one picture on one side and another picture, upside down, on the reverse side. String is threaded through the holes, twist the string and then jerk it taut to set it spinning and the two pictures will be superimposed on one another. The favourite with the Victorians was a bird on one side and a cage on the other. I have used here a man on one side and a penny farthing bicycle on the other. See if you can get him to ride it. Use ⅛in (4mm) or ¼in (6mm) ply.

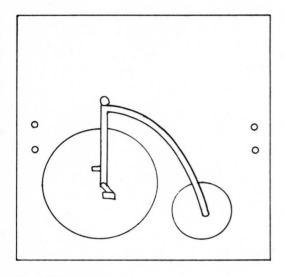

Fig 2 Thaumatrope

Acrobat
This acrobat works by adjusting the tension of the string by squeezing and releasing the bottom of the frame.

1 Cut out the body and the thighs from ½in (12mm) ply (fig 3).
2 Cut out the arms and legs from ¼in (6mm) ply.
3 Drill two small holes through both the hands for the string to pass through.
4 Drill two ⁵⁄₁₆in (8mm) holes right through the body for the arms and the thighs.
5 Drill ¼in (6mm) holes in the arms and thighs but do not drill right the way through, use adhesive tape wrapped around the drill bit as a depth gauge.

6 Drill a hole in each of the legs just large enough for the size of screw you are going to use to pass through freely.
7 Cut two lengths of 12×½×½in (305× 12×12mm) ply and drill two small holes in the top of each for the string (fig 4).
8 Drill a ¼in (6mm) hole in each length of wood 3in (75mm) from the bottom and fit a 3in (75mm) length of dowel as a cross-piece.
9 Paint the framework and the acrobat.
10 Cut a length of dowel to pass through the body and glue the arms on to the ends of it. Do the same for the thighs.
11 Use a round-headed screw to fix the legs to the thighs.
12 Fit the string making sure to twist it, as shown in fig 4.

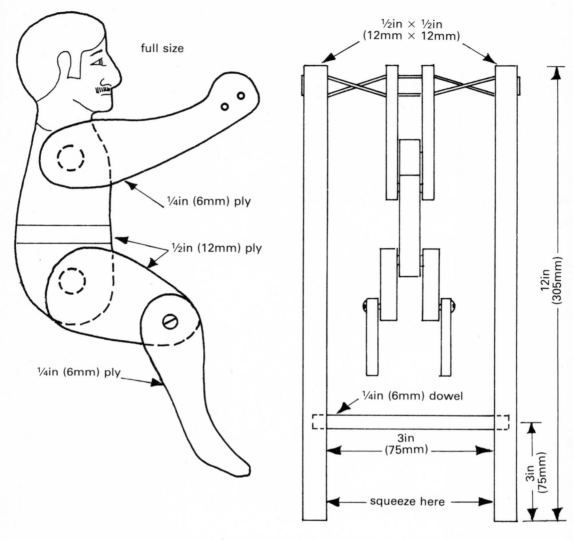

full size

¼in (6mm) ply

½in (12mm) ply

¼in (6mm) ply

½in × ½in
(12mm × 12mm)

12in
(305mm)

¼in (6mm) dowel

3in
(75mm)

3in
(75mm)

squeeze here

Fig 3 Body of acrobat showing moving arms and legs

Fig 4 Front view of acrobat and frame

Gymnast

This is a very simple toy to make and once he is started in motion he will roll right along the bars.

1 Cut out the gymnast from a ¼in (6mm) ply (fig 5).

2 Drill a ⅛in (4mm) hole through his hands and pass a 3½in (87mm) length of ⅛in (4mm) dowel through it.

3 Cut out a piece of 8½×3¼×¼in (216× 81×6mm) ply for the base and drill four holes for the ½in (12mm) dowel uprights (fig 6).

4 Cut out four 3½in (87mm) lengths of ½in (12mm) dowel (fig 7), and using the fretsaw (jigsaw) cut a notch ¼in (6mm) wide × ¼in (6mm) deep for the parallel bars (fig 8).

5 Glue the posts and bars in place.

6 Paint the gymnast and the bars. It is best not to use gloss paint for the gymnast's pole or the bars, but if you do, it is possible to roughen them with sandpaper.

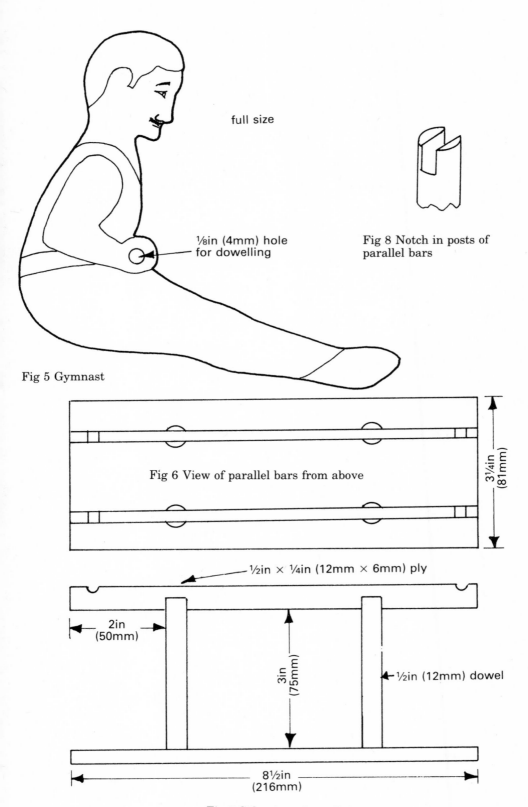

full size

⅛in (4mm) hole
for dowelling

Fig 8 Notch in posts of
parallel bars

Fig 5 Gymnast

Fig 6 View of parallel bars from above

3¼in
(81mm)

½in × ¼in (12mm × 6mm) ply

2in
(50mm)

3in
(75mm)

½in (12mm) dowel

8½in
(216mm)

Fig 7 Side view of parallel bars

Clown

When you place the clown at the top of the pegboard he bounces from one peg to the next until he finds his way down. This really is an easy toy to make; my daughter made one at primary school when she was about six. I think she used a hand drill rather than an electric drill for safety reasons, and the teacher marked the position of the pegs.

2¼in (57mm)

1in (25mm)

2in (50mm)

2in (50mm)

22in (558mm)

3in (75mm)

3¼in (81mm)

Fig 10 Board and peg positions

Fig 9 Clown

1 Cut out the clown from ¼in (6mm) ply (fig 9).
2 Cut out a piece of ¼in (6mm), ⅜in (9mm) or ½in (12mm) ply to a size of 22×3¼in (558×81mm) for the board (fig 10).
3 Mark out the position of the pegs and drill ¼in (6mm) holes.
4 Cut ten 1in lengths of ¼in (6mm) dowel and glue them in the holes.
5 Paint the clown and the board.

INDEX